THE FOUR AGES OF TSURAI

THE FOUR
A DOCUMENTARY HISTORY OF THE
AGES OF
INDIAN VILLAGE ON TRINIDAD BAY
TSURAI

Robert F. Heizer and John E. Mills

Translations of Spanish Documents by Donald C. Cutter

UNIVERSITY OF CALIFORNIA PRESS

BERKELEY AND LOS ANGELES » 1952

UNIVERSITY OF CALIFORNIA PRESS
Berkeley and Los Angeles
California

CAMBRIDGE UNIVERSITY PRESS
London, England

Copyright, 1952, by
THE REGENTS OF THE UNIVERSITY OF CALIFORNIA

by the University of California Press

Designed by Adrian Wilson

PREFACE

BEFORE *the coming of the white man, the Yurok Indians of northwestern California inhabited the banks of the Klamath River below the mouth of the Trinity, and the ocean shore for some distance north and south of the mouth of the Klamath. The total population of the tribe at the time the white men came to this coast was about 2,500. The Yurok lived, according to information secured from the natives, in fifty-four towns stretching along both banks of the Klamath River and the ocean front. The southernmost of these towns, on the shore of Trinidad Bay, was named Tsurai. It is this village and its occupants whose history, imperfectly though it is recorded, forms the content of this book.*

The authors wish to thank Dr. Donald Cutter, Assistant Professor, Department of History, University of Southern California, for translating from the Spanish the several accounts of the Hezeta expedition. The Bancroft Library of the University of California, through its Director, Dr. George P. Hammond, made available the rich facilities of its source collection for much of the data contained in the present work.

To the Institute of Social Sciences, University of California, Berkeley, and its Director, Dean W. R. Dennes, we gratefully acknowledge two subventions (Project 81) which helped defray the cost of illustrations, translations, and preparation of the manuscript. The Committee on Research, under the chairmanship of Professor R. T. Birge, financed the archaeological work at Trinidad Bay in 1949 through Anthropology Research Grant No. 217.

We thank Mr. Earl Hallmark, Mr. Fred Hauck, and Mr. Ray Walker of Eureka for permission to conduct archaeological explorations on their property, which includes the site of the former village of Tsurai.

To many California Indian friends, notably Mr. and Mrs. Axel

Lindgren, Miss Olive Franks, Mrs. Minnie Shaffer of Trinidad, and Mr. Robert Spott of Requa, we reaffirm here our mutual interest in the native history of the people of Trinidad Bay.

Professor Alfred L. Kroeber, dean of California anthropologists, has read the manuscript of this work and has offered valuable suggestions.

Permission to reproduce copyrighted materials in J. Goldsborough Bruff's Gold Rush *has been granted by the Columbia University Press, the Stirling Library of Yale University, and the editors, Georgia W. Read and Ruth Gaines. The California Historical Society has granted permission to reprint parts of the accounts of Archibald Menzies, Francisco de Eliza, and Ernest de Massey. To all these institutions and persons we express our thanks.*

R. F. H. and J. E. M.

Berkeley, California

CONTENTS

	INTRODUCTION	1
I	THE PREHISTORY OF TSURAI	7
II	DISCOVERY AND EXPLORATION, 1775–1800	19
	Journal of Don Juan Francisco de la Bodega y Quadra	21
	Journal of Don Bruno de Hezeta	29
	Diary of Fray Miguel de la Campa	38
	Journal of Don Francisco Antonio Mourelle	45
	Diary of Don Juan Pérez	53
	Act of Possession of the Spanish Crown at Trinidad Bay, June 11, 1775	57
	Trinidad Bay from the Journal of Archibald Menzies	61
	Extract from the Journal of Captain George Vancouver	63
	Extract of the Account of the Voyage of the Spanish Brigantine Activo *under the Command of Lieutenant Don Francisco de Eliza*	68
III	EXPLOITATION: THE FUR TRADE, 1800–1849	73
	Experiences of William Shaler and the Crew of the Lelia Byrd	75
	Visit of Captain Jonathan Winship, Jr., to Trinidad Bay	82
	Visit of the Brig Columbia, *Captain John Jennings, to Trinidad Bay, from the Journal of Peter Corney*	84
IV	DECLINE AND FALL: THE AMERICAN INVASION, 1850–1916	105
	Trinidad Bay in 1849 from L. K. Wood's Account of the Josiah Gregg Expedition	107

H. D. la Motte's Account of Trinidad Bay	108
The Trinidad Bay Indians after the Rediscovery of the Bay by Sea and the Founding of Trinidad City, from Ernest de Massey's Account	109
Remarks on Trinidad Indians by J. Goldsborough Bruff	113
Carl Meyer's Account of the Indians of Trinidad Bay	119
Baron Karl von Loeffelholz's Account of the Tsorei Indians of Trinidad Bay	135
Tsurai Village, 1851–1916	180
APPENDIX: INDIAN PLACE NAMES IN TRINIDAD BAY	185
NOTES	193

ILLUSTRATIONS

Plates

1	*Aerial View of Trinidad Bay from the South*	85
2	*Prehistoric and Historic Indian Implements*	86
3	*Bow and Arrows of the Trinidad Bay Indians*	87
4	*Aerial View of Tsurai Village and Site Area*	88
5	*View of Trinidad Bay from the East Shore*	89
6	*Pages from the Act of Possession of the Spanish Crown, Trinidad Bay, June 11, 1775*	90
7	*Graveyard and House, Tsurai Village, 1851*	91
8	*Grave and Sweathouse, Tsurai Village, 1851*	92
9	*Plank Houses, Tsurai Village, 1851*	93
10	*Willie Childs, a Last Survivor of Tsurai, about 1900*	94

Figures

1	*Archaeological Objects of Stone, Bone, and Shell from Tsurai*	10
2	*Archaeological Objects of Bone, Steatite, and Elk Antler from Tsurai*	12
3	*Historic Trade Articles from Tsurai and Objects Collected at Trinidad Bay by Vancouver, 1793*	15

MAPS

1 *Waterman's Plan of Tsurai Village about 1906*   95
2 *The Hezeta Map of Trinidad Bay, 1775*   96
3 *Vancouver's Chart of Trinidad Bay, 1793*   97
4 *United States Coast Survey Map of Trinidad Bay, 1851*   98
5 *Contour Map of Tsurai Village Area Showing Location of Houses and Owners' Names, about 1900*   99
6 *Map of Trinidad Bay Showing Locations of Places with Indian Names*   100

INTRODUCTION

In all California no Indian village and its inhabitants has been as fully described by early explorers and traders as *Tsurai* ("mountain") on Trinidad Bay at 124° 8½′ W. longitude and 41° 03′ N. latitude.

The discovery of Trinidad Bay is probably to be attributed to Sebastian Rodriguez Cermeño, Portuguese captain of the ill-fated *San Agustin,* which in November, 1595, entered the bay but did not anchor for fear of rocks.[1] H. R. Wagner is the chief proponent of the theory that Sir Francis Drake anchored in Trinidad Bay in June, 1579,[2] but this view of the location of Drake's landfall is almost certainly incorrect.[3]

The significant history of Trinidad Bay begins in 1775 when Spanish explorers in the frigate *Santiago,* Captain Don Bruno de Hezeta, and the schooner *Sonora,* Captain Don Juan Francisco de la Bodega y Quadra, spent about a week there. A number of accounts of the Indians, written by officers in charge and ships' chaplains, have been preserved, and five of these (by Hezeta, Mourelle, de la Campa, Pérez, and Bodega) are reproduced here.

In May, 1793, Captain George Vancouver in the *Discovery* remained in Trinidad Bay for a few days taking on fresh water and observing the natives. Both Vancouver's journal and one kept by the naturalist Archibald Menzies yield observations on the village and people of the bay.

In August, 1793, the Spanish brigantine *Activo* took on water and wood in Trinidad Bay, and Lieutenant Don Francisco de Eliza's account of his brief sojourn contains some facts of interest.

By 1800 the Northwest Coast fur trade was in full swing, and trading ships from half a dozen nations were actively exchanging cloth, glass, and metal objects with coastal Indians for precious sea-otter furs. At what date it became known that Trinidad Bay was one of the favorite haunts of the sea otter,[4] and the bay became a port of call of European trading ships, may only be conjectured.

1

William Shaler in the *Lelia Byrd,* a fur-trading ship sailing between China and Northwest Coast ports, spent a week in Trinidad Bay in May, 1804.

In June, 1806, Jonathan Winship Jr. in the *O'Cain* was in Trinidad Bay and had trouble with the Indians. He avoided a serious fight by withdrawing, but not before one of the Indians of the bay was killed. The international nature of the sea-otter fur trade is vividly attested by this incident. The *O'Cain* was American owned, but sailing under Russian contract; she carried Aleutian Island natives as hunters, and at this time was in Spanish territory carrying on trade with American Indians.

Adele Ogden in her excellent work on the sea-otter trade has noted that the following vessels visited Trinidad Bay for trading purposes between 1808 and 1817:[5] in 1808, the ship *Kodiak,* Captain Petrov, owner, Russian American Company, forty crew men, and one hundred and thirty Northwest Coast Indian hunters and twenty Northwest Coast women on board;[6] in 1808 the ship *Mercury*, Captain George Washington Eayers, Boston owners, sailing under Russian contract; in 1810, the ship *Albatross,* Captain Nathan Winship, Boston owners, sailing under Russian contract; in 1817, the brig *Columbia,* Captain John Jennings, owner, Northwest Company. An account of the *Columbia*'s visit written by Peter Corney, first officer, shows that the traders were having trouble with the Indians, and that the latter well understood the power of a musket. Corney mentions that a Spanish cross, presumably the one erected by the Hezeta party forty-two years before, was still to be seen.

Although the fur trade continued for some years, either Trinidad was not visited often after 1817, or documentary evidence of contacts with the Indians of that bay has been lost, or is yet unknown. Eugène Duflot de Mofras may have visited Trinidad Bay in 1841 to judge from his description of the bay. His map of the bay is obviously a direct copy of Vancouver's drawn nearly fifty years before.[7] Dr. Owen C. Coy refers to the expedition by ship of William G. Ray, factor of the Hudson's Bay Company, who probably visited Trinidad Bay in 1830 or 1831.[8]

The next event of importance was the activity of placer gold

INTRODUCTION

miners in 1850 along the Trinity River, a main affluent of the Klamath River. Trinidad Bay became the supply and debarkation port for the Argonauts on their way to the Trinity placers. Of the many journals of this period which doubtless exist, we have found only four of particular interest for this book. The first, written by a Frenchman, Ernest de Massey, is a penetrating sketch of the native people of Trinidad Bay in 1850, the year when they were swamped by the Caucasian "invasion." A brief but illuminating second account, by J. Goldsborough Bruff, is most valuable because of the excellent illustrations of the Tsurai village which he drew on the spot. The third, by Carl Meyer, is a detailed and remarkably objective account of life and times of the period (1851) in the Indian village at Trinidad Bay. The fourth account is a straight anthropological sketch, written by Baron Hans von Loeffelholz and his son Karl. Meyer calls Hans von Loeffelholz the first white settler, and the latter's observations were made between 1850 and 1856; the document itself is not later than 1857.

Our résumé of the history of known Caucasian contacts with the Trinidad Indians may be summarized by the observation that three periods are represented: one, the exploration era (1775–1800) when contacts with white men were occasional and friendly; two, the fur-trade period (*ca.* 1800–*ca.* 1849) when relations between the white traders and the natives had deteriorated to ever-present hostility and mutual suspicion; and three, the American period (1850–1916) marked initially by the Trinity gold rush and terminally by the final abandonment of Tsurai village. The white man's treatment of the northwestern Indians in this last period[*] was similar to that experienced by the Sierran and Valley tribes as related in detail by S. F. Cook.[1]

This compilation of documents is of value from several viewpoints. First, they are admittedly selected for their ethnographic detail and as such constitute a documentary record of the culture and recent history of the southern coast Yurok Indians. The accounts are also of historical importance and will, we hope, prove useful to readers interested in the coastal explorations, the fur trade, and the history of Trinidad Bay itself. They stand out primarily, however, as eyewitness records of the decline and disappearance of a pre-Caucasian civilization which we, after effecting its destruction, have learned to appreciate and to regard as important to the cultural background of the state.

It may be further noted that several of the main currents of northwest Pacific history converge here among the simple Indian folk of Trinidad Bay. No effect, however small, was registered upon the ponderous course of events set in motion by the European powers of Spain, England, Russia and France, and the growing American nation by the several visits to and ultimate settlement of Trinidad, yet the people of Tsurai village may be counted as having played a part in the Spanish exploration of the North Pacific, in the historically significant international fur trade on the Northwest Coast, and in the great California Gold Rush. If it is important, as time, persons, and events become the past and the stuff of history, that a nation may not be forgotten, then the people of Tsurai have earned their place in our heritage.

The authors desire here to suggest that slight effort by local residents could be effective in causing the state to set aside the village area as a historic site and thus to prevent its destruction by relic collectors and real-estate activities. Surely a place which has seen the ships of the Spanish crown, of the English crown, of the adventurous sea-otter fur traders, and of the lusty Argonauts bound for the Trinity placers deserves protection for future Californians. The village site area is rich in archaeological materials, and among these are objects secured by the Indians from each of the various Caucasian explorers and traders who entered Trinidad Bay. The rapidly growing interest in and appreciation of the importance of California's diminishing number of archaeological sites will insure, in due time, the expert archaeological investigation of those which can be saved now from destruction. The present authors would place the significance of the Tsurai site as of the highest rank and urge that a forward-looking local group or the state take steps to preserve this unique repository of California history.

1

THE PREHISTORY OF TSURAI

THE PREHISTORY OF TSURAI

During the summer of 1949 the Department of Anthropology of the University of California undertook an archaeological exploration of the long-abandoned village of Tsurai in an effort to determine what the ancient history of its occupation had been. This effort was reasonably successful, and in the following pages the prehistoric culture will be outlined.

The area occupied by the former village is now thickly overgrown with nettles, ash, and pepperwood trees. The entire area from the beach to the bluff and between the two small creeks (map 1) was covered to some depth with occupation refuse or "midden" deposit. This stratum consisted of all the materials and objects which the occupants of the village had thrown away or lost. It was, in fact, a huge refuse dump consisting of earth, mussel and clam shells, elk, seal, and sea-lion bones, stones once used for boiling food in baskets or for house construction, ashes from fires, sand layers which had once been housefloors, and broken and whole implements of stone, bone, and shell. Such refuse heaps or middens are usual in former California Indian village sites, and they result from the simple process of tossing all unwanted materials outside the door. During the course of years and centuries, the amount and thickness of the accumulated refuse may become very considerable. Refuse accumulations as much as thirty feet in depth have been recorded for sites on the shore of San Francisco Bay.

The archaeologist, whom someone called "a scientist who rummages in the garbage heaps of antiquity," has developed very careful and precise techniques of excavation. He does not simply dig a hole, or try to excavate as much as is physically possible, but works carefully with a spade, a small trowel, and whiskbroom so that everything he uncovers will be accompanied by accurate location and depth measurements. In this way he transfers to notebooks and maps exact information on the placement of every object found so that its position is known in relation to all other objects in the deposit. Then, with these facts, the archaeologist proceeds to reconstruct the process by which the refuse deposits were built up, and in so doing can often point to one group of artifacts which belongs to the earliest period of occupation, to another which may be assigned a later date, and so on until he is reasonably sure that the chronological sequence of implements in different strata has been determined. A simplified illustration of this method may be seen in the gross vertical stratification exhibited in the Tsurai deposits where the uppermost levels contain metal objects, glass, and crockery obtained from the white man, and the lower levels where such items are absent. Since 1850 marks the date when appreciable quantities of European-made objects became accessible to the Indians, we may be sure that all objects in the historic level are post-1850, and the objects found below this level and lying in undisturbed soil are pre-1850 in time.

We have assumed that the historic level, which is delimited by the occurrence of an abundance of white man's dishes, bottles, and metal objects, began to be laid down in 1850 when Trinidad became the debarkation point for the Trinity River gold placers, and was completed in 1916 when the village was abandoned by the natives. The diagrams of stratigraphic profiles and field notes written during the excavation have been carefully studied, and the ratio of depths of the historic level to the prehistoric levels calculated. For example, in a given spot, the historic level (1850–1916) may be twelve inches in depth, and the pre-1850 level thirty-six inches in depth, the ratio being one to three. In this instance the prehistoric level would be one hundred and ninety-eight years old if we assume that the refuse layers accumulated at the same rate after 1850 as before that date. With a large number of such ratios of relative depth, we have calculated that the site of Tsurai was first occupied about A.D. 1620. The village would have been one hundred and fifty-five years old when discovered by the Hezeta expedition in 1775, two hundred and thirty-one years old when seen by Bruff in 1851, and two hundred and ninety-six years old when abandoned in 1916. If Cermeño was actually in Trinidad Bay in 1595, he would not, according to our computation, have seen the Tsurai village. The Indian inhabitants of the bay at that date may have occupied the prehistoric site about five hundred yards south along the shore. This we named the Kidder site after its present owner. Our reason for suggesting that this prehistoric site may be older than Tsurai rests upon the fact that the recent Indians of Trinidad do not remember the name of this ancient site and have a tradition that when the first Tsurai people came to settle Trinidad, they found already resident at the Kidder site a small population which they drove out toward the south. This kind of history is more likely to be myth than fact, yet some tradition of the founding of an important village three centuries before could conceivably be remembered in essential fact. Excavation of the Kidder site would solve this problem.

It is certain that the entire occupation of the Tsurai village is contemporaneous with the culture called "late prehistoric and historic." The excavation of a large shellmound at Patrick's Point State Park by the University of California in 1948 resulted in the identification of two prehistoric cultures called early prehistoric and late prehistoric. Since local Indians living in 1908 could not remember the name of the village at Patrick's Point, and since we found no evidence of its habitation by a group in the 1850's, the conclusion was that the site had been abandoned before 1850 and perhaps as early as 1800. The culture disclosed in the lower levels of the Patrick's Point shellmound, although similar to that from the upper levels, did differ in certain specific features to the extent that we felt justified in establishing two cultural phases which were assigned the time-difference terms of early and late. Referring to our earlier calculation of the antiquity of the Tsurai site, we suggest that the late prehistoric period along this part of the Humboldt County coast is at least three hundred and fifty years old. The culture sequence in the Trinidad Bay–Patrick's Point area may be summarized in the following table:

DATES	PATRICK'S POINT SITE	TSURAI SITE	OTHER SITES
A.D. 1850	(Absent)	Full historic	
A.D. ± ? 1600	Late prehistoric	Late prehistoric and early historic	Dry Lagoon site
A.D. ? 1000	Early prehistoric	(Absent)	Kidder site

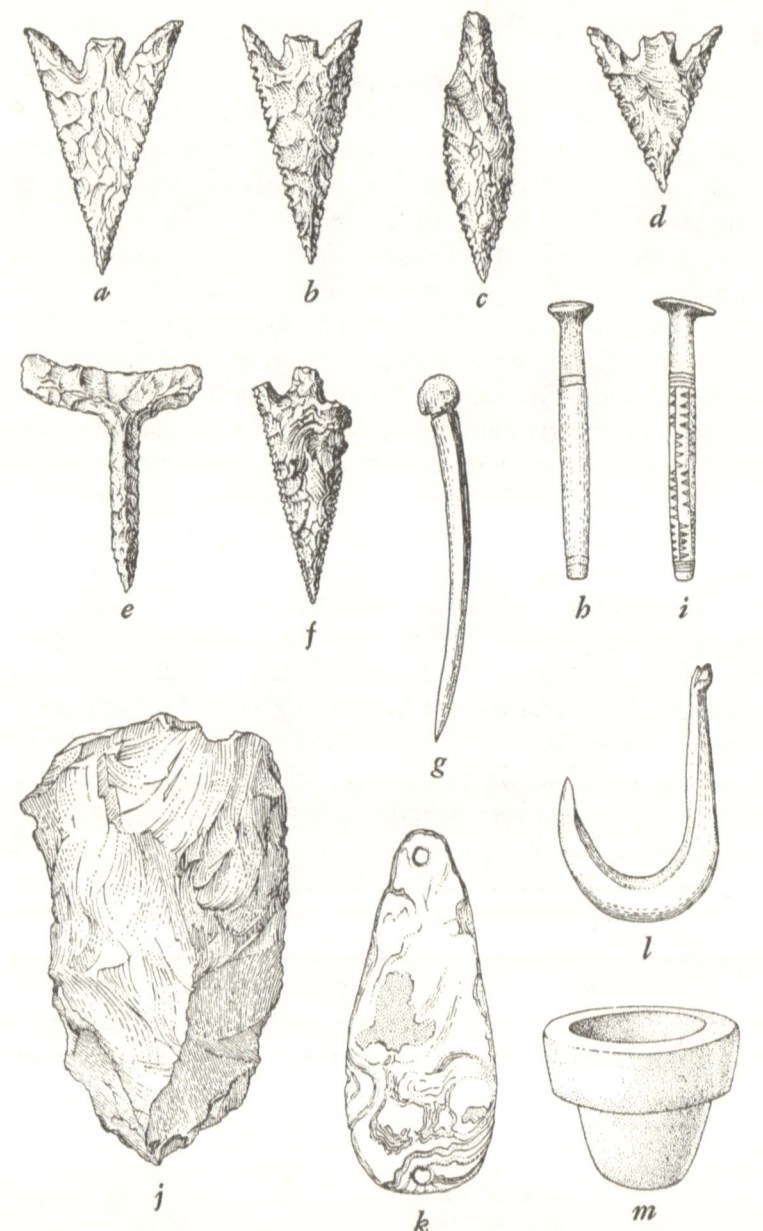

Fig. 1. Archaeological Objects of Stone, Bone, and Shell from Tsurai.

The Prehistory of Tsurai

The "other sites" were not occupied in historic times, according to Indian testimony; our assignment of these sites to prehistoric culture periods is based on inference and is wholly tentative.

The native artifacts from the late prehistoric levels represent only those made of rot-resistant materials such as stone, shell, and bone. Wooden objects which were important in the material culture of the recent Indians of northwestern California have, of course, long since disintegrated in the moist refuse layers.

From the bones of sea mammals (seal, sea lion, killed with barbed harpoons; see fig. 2, *a–b*) were made blunt-ended flint chipping tools (fig. 2, *c*) which were used, in the manner described by Loeffelholz, to fashion flint arrow points (fig. 1) and the stone tips for the sea-lion harpoons, and drills (fig. 1, *e*). Elk were hunted, not only for their flesh, but for their hides which were cleaned with flint scrapers (fig. 1, *j*), and for their bones and antlers, from which harpoons, ornaments (figs. 1, *h–i*), awls and punches (figs. 2, *d–e, g–j*), and other tools were made.

Stone was used for making mortars with a shallow grinding basin (pl. 2, *h–i*), on top of which was set a twined basketry hopper. Long cylindrical stone pestles tapering to a point at the handle end and with a raised ring near the pounding end (pl. 2, *g*) were used with the hopper mortars to crush acorns into flour. Curved stone adze handles to which were lashed cutting blades of shell or stone (pl. 2, *f*) were used to excavate the interiors and shape the sides of redwood canoes.

Antler wedges with thin tips and battered polls were found in quantity and attest the ancient presence of split redwood planks used in house construction. Bell-shaped mauls, laboriously pecked from beach boulders and well polished from use, occurred in the refuse layers at Tsurai, but they were invariably broken specimens (pl. 2, *e*) which had been thrown away by their former owners. These mauls were used like acorn-grinding pestles, the flat-bottom surface being the hammering end to drive antler wedges into redwood logs to split off planks.

One particular stone called steatite, a variety of soapstone which is dark blue in color, soft, easily worked, and capable of receiving

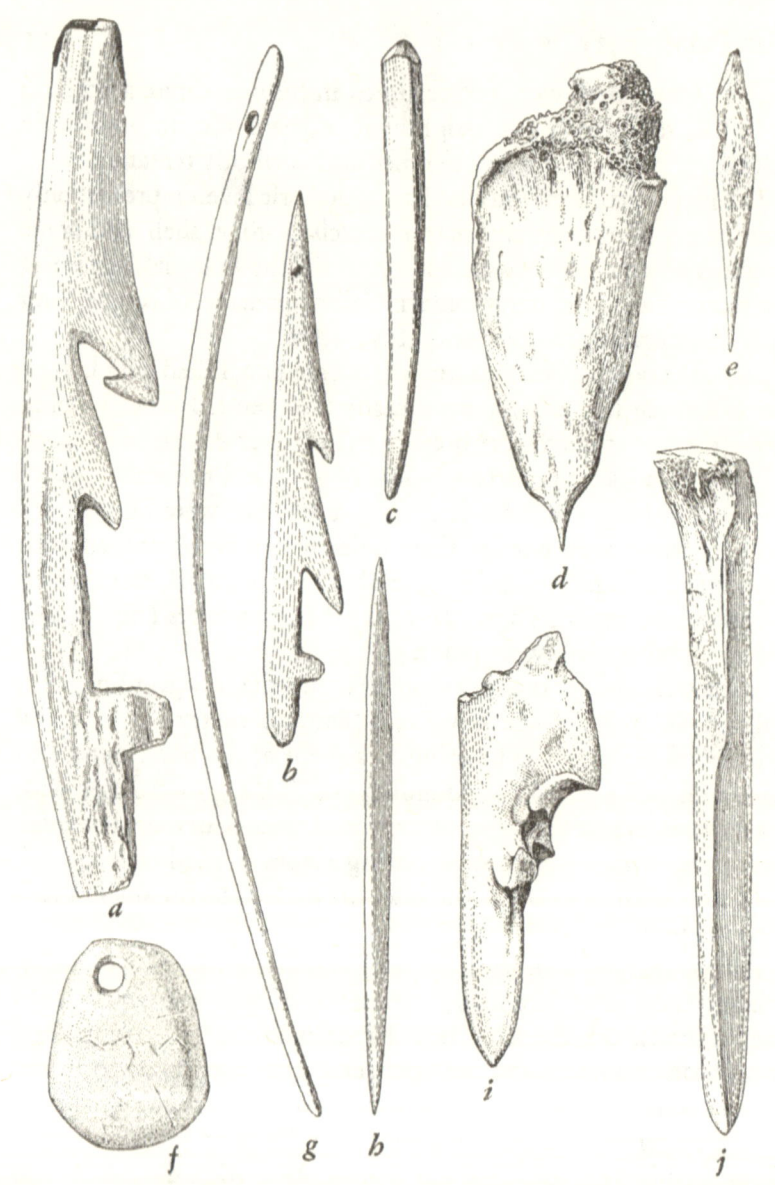

Fig. 2. Archaeological Objects of Bone, Steatite, and Elkhorn from Tsurai.

The Prehistory of Tsurai

a high polish, was much used. The source of this material is about one mile down the beach from Tsurai at locus no. 45 on map 6, page 100. From steatite were made ornaments (fig. 2, *f*) and bowls for tobacco pipes which were affixed to the ends of wooden stems (fig. 1, *m*). To catch the grease of salmon and seal which were cured by smoking, the former inhabitants of Tsurai used round or oval bowls of steatite. Some steatite vessels are too small to have served as dripping pans, and may have been toys; some of the steatite vessels were made in imitation of the redwood canoe with its squared ends and flat bottom. Steatite has peculiar qualities for withstanding heat, a feature which accounts for its use as tobacco pipe bowls and as rocks used in the stone boiling process described by De Massey.

Some aspects of the economy of the ancient Tsurai people can be recovered from archaeology. Thus the great abundance of bivalve shells tells us that mussels (*Mytilus californianus*), cockles (*Cardium corbis*), and clams (*Saxidomus nuttali*), razor shell (*Siliqua patula*), and rock oyster (*Hinnites multirugosus*) were important dietary resources. Abalones (*Haliotis rufescens*), sea urchins (*Strongylocentrotus purpuratus*), sea snails (*Polinices lewisii*), and barnacles from the sea helped fill the larder. Fish bones were abundant, and it may be supposed that rockfish and salmon comprise the bulk of these remains. Bones of the Roosevelt elk (*Cervus rooseveltii*), seal (*Phoca callorhinus*), and sea lion (*Eumotopia jubata*) were very common and probably furnished the main meat and fat resources, together with white-tailed deer (*Odocoileus virginianus*) and raccoon (*Procyon lotor*). Acorns were used, if we are correct in assigning a function to the stone mortars (pl. 2, *h–i*), and pestles (pl. 2, *g*), and various edible roots, bulbs, and berries must have been eaten. Bones of the sea otter (*Enhydra* sp.) are fairly common, and we know from the accounts of the early visitors to Trinidad Bay that these animals were hunted for their superior fur.

No evidence was found during the excavation of the site of the visit of the Hezeta expedition to Trinidad Bay in 1775. Any beads, glass objects, or metal tools given by the Spaniards to the Indians were probably either buried with the dead or were discarded when broken or worn out. Such items must have been distributed by the white men in rather small quantity, and our failure to find them is understandable. No graves were found or excavated by the University expedition.

The fur-trade period is attested by a few archaeological specimens which include the base of an amethyst glass vase or lamp, made in Sandwich, Cape Cod (pl. 2, *j*). This glass probably dates from about 1825. It was discovered in a cache of aboriginal objects (pl. 1, *e*) lying at the bottom of a plank-lined storage pit dug through a house-floor. The iron swords mentioned in several accounts are represented by several examples (pl. 2, *k*). One is the handle end and part of the blade and bears deep rectangular notches along the edge at the end.[1] This notching occurs on a similar sword (pl. 2, *c–d*) collected nearly fifty years ago from Yurok tribal members who, at that time, retained these swords as heirlooms handed down to them from ancestors. These swords probably date from the 1800–1850 period and were made by ships' armorers from iron stock to serve as trade goods in securing the valuable furs of the sea otter. Other trade items of this sort are the C-shaped iron wire, and copper bracelets and rings (fig. 3).

The uppermost stratum of refuse deposit at the Tsurai site contained large numbers of broken objects obtained from white men. A large quantity of this material is obviously of mid-nineteenth-century date and constitutes the tangible remains of the period about 1850 when Trinidad Bay was the anchoring spot of sailing ships and steamers loaded with goods and passengers for the gold fields of the Trinity River. Glass bottles, fragments of porcelain and chinaware, a variety of metal scrap, and the like fall into this class. The top few inches contain similar materials but of still more recent date, and can be distinguished from the earlier historic material by the types of glass bottles and otherwise modified materials introduced by whitemen to produce familiar native forms. The old food sources mentioned above continued to be used, but tin cans, bottles, and bones of domestic cattle and pigs show that the native dietary was expanded through contact with white men. Elk and deer bones are noticeably more abundant in the historic level, and it may be suggested that the acquisition of rifles by the Indians made these animals an easier

The Prehistory of Tsurai

target than formerly, when snares and the bow and arrow were the only means of capture. In the historic level there is apparent also an increase in numbers of worked steatite objects relative to the pre-1850 levels. This increase is due no doubt to the availability of metal-pointed chisels made from files, which are effective implements for

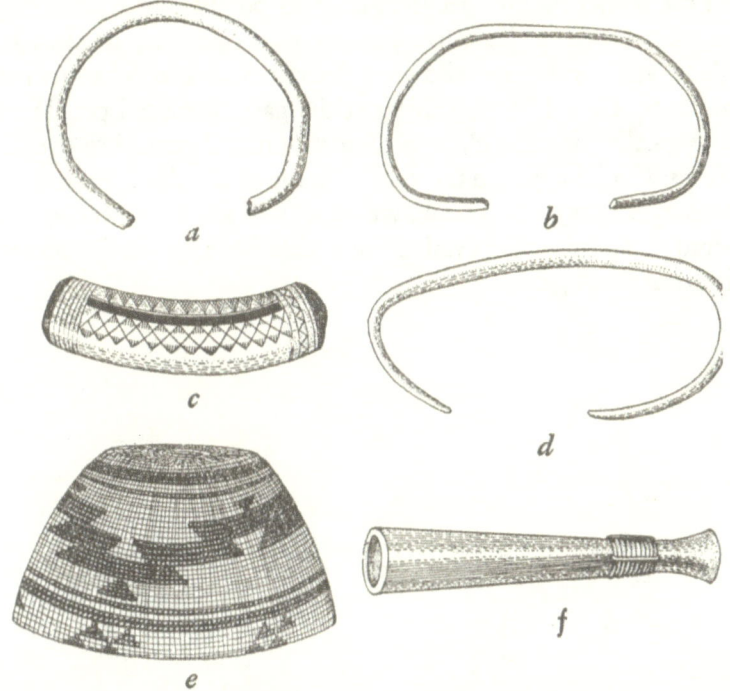

Fig. 3. Historic Trade Articles from Tsurai and Objects Collected by Vancouver, 1793. *a, b, d,* copper and iron bracelets secured from traders; *c,* elkhorn dentalia purse collected at Trinidad Bay by Vancouver expedition, 1793, now in the British Museum; *e,* twined, decorated woman's basketry hat, collected by Vancouver expedition, 1793; *f,* tubular stone pipe wrapped with sinew, collected by Vancouver expedition, 1793.

working the soft steatite. Similarly, the metal ax, hatchet, and saw made the making of planks much easier, though this effect on the native woodworking complex may have lasted only until sawed lumber from local mills or abandoned houses was available for salvage. In 1906, for example, there remained only one house (Old Mau's) which was Indian in plan, construction, and materials, the others being unelaborate frame buildings.

The cumulative effect on the people and civilization of Tsurai of contact with the white man was the abandonment of the village and the scattering and decimation of its population. Although in 1949 there were at least five persons who had once lived in the village, and forty more who were direct descendants of former inhabitants, the old life is a thing of the past. Some old people still nostalgically visit the old site on occasion and reminisce over incidents which happened there, but Tsurai itself is dead, and even its memory is dying. This book, we hope, will aid in preserving that memory and making it available as a record of a part of California's historical heritage.

II
DISCOVERY AND EXPLORATION
1775-1800

DISCOVERY AND EXPLORATION
1775-1800

SPANISH fears of Russian designs in the North Pacific led the Viceroy of Mexico, Antonio María de Bucareli y Ursúa, to dispatch a sea expedition from San Blas in January, 1774, to explore the northwestern coasts. The ship was the *Santiago,* Juan Pérez, captain. In March, 1775, regular officers of the Spanish navy continued the explorations with a view to selecting sites for possible settlement, making coastal charts, and reporting on the natives, fauna, flora, minerals, and the like. The 1775 expedition was commanded by Don Bruno de Hezeta who was also captain of the frigate *Santiago.* The schooner *Sonora,* Don Juan Francisco de la Bodega y Quadra, captain, was taken as consort ship to survey in shallow shore waters. The expedition effected the first landing of Europeans on the Northwest Coast at Cape Grenville (latitude 47° 20′) and discovered the mouth of the Columbia River. The ships entered a bay which they named Trinidad, on June 9, 1775, and remained there until June 19. A number of diaries or official journals of the expedition were kept, and extracts of those of Hezeta, commander of the expedition, Bodega, captain of the *Sonora,* Fray Miguel de la Campa, chaplain of the *Santiago,* Pérez, vice commander of the *Santiago,* and Don Francisco Antonio Mourelle, second pilot of the *Sonora,* are printed here.[1] Although generally similar, these several accounts vary in details.

Captain George Vancouver had been in California in 1792 with the *Discovery* and *Chatham* after meeting Bodega at Nootka Sound, Vancouver Island, in an unsuccessful effort to settle the question of the ownership of that port. Vancouver returned in 1793, arriving at Trinidad Bay, May 2. After gathering firewood and filling his water casks, he sailed for the Northwest Coast on the morning of May 5.

The accounts of Trinidad Bay in the journals of Archibald Menzies, naturalist of the expedition, and of Vancouver, the commander, are printed here.

The North Pacific exploration of Don Francisco de Eliza in 1793 was for the purpose of compiling an accurate hydrographic chart of the coast.[2] This expedition marks the close of the brief period of Spanish exploring activity in the far north. The Spaniards had many matters with which to occupy themselves farther south in Mexico and California and left the settlement and fur trade in the North Pacific to other nations.[3]

JOURNAL OF DON JUAN FRANCISCO DE LA BODEGA Y QUADRA, CAPTAIN OF THE SCHOONER SONORA, AT TRINIDAD BAY, JUNE 9-19, 1775

AFTER they rounded the point [Trinidad Head] to enter the port they saw many Indian canoes coming from the north. The natives approached the frigate, with whose crew they immediately traded skins for trifles which were offered them. While the trading was going on they saw a small village on the shore and some of the villagers walking along the beach. After exploring the port they found they could anchor near the shore. They did this immediately, fastening the cables to some rocks that were suitable for this purpose.

Let us note here that, although the French chart[4] shows some large bays, the coast we discovered is rather straight without any bays which can be distinguished. According to the chart the party must be at Cape Fortuna, and it is possible that this was the name given to the mountain [Trinidad Head] that formed this port.

On the eleventh the commandant took possession of those lands with all the dignity and solemnity that the accomodations of the port afforded, Mass was celebrated, a sermon was preached, and many volleys of cannon and guns were fired as an act of thanks to the Creator. The Indians were terrified by these noises. After recovering, the natives made another visit to the ship. All believed that those volleys could demolish the near-by mountains.[5]

"Segunda exploracion de la Costa septentrional de la California en 1775 con la Fragata Santiago y la Goleta Sonora, mandados p^r el Ten^{te} de Navio D. Bruno de Hecata, y el de Fragata D. Juan de la Cuadra desde el P^{to} de S^n Blás n^{ta} 58 g^s de latitud." Academia de la Historia, 12-26-4-D-91, Madrid. Bodega also composed a summary of the expedition entitled "Comento de la Navegacion y descubrimt^{os} hechos en los Viages de Orden de S.M. en la Costa Septentrional de California, desde la Latitud de 21 gr^s 30 min^{os} en que se halla el Departam^{to} de S^n Blás, por D^n Juan Franc^{co} de la Bodega y Cuadra del Orden de S^{n}Tiago y Captain de Navio de la RI Armada." This document is now in the Depósito Hidrográfico, Madrid, letra d 3^a; there is a typescript copy in the Bancroft Library of the University of California, Berkeley.

The port was given the name "La Santisima Trinidad," because possession was taken on the feast day of the Holy Trinity.

On the following days the men continued the tasks of gathering wood, ballast, and water, and making topmasts from the pines to carry as spares.

Then they carefully set about observing the society of the inhabitants, their way of life, habits, dress, cleanliness, dwellings, religious rites, language, arms (which they especially desire), hunting, fishing, and the occurrence of metals, precious stones, or other worthwhile minerals; but the short time the ship remained here was not sufficient for us to establish these important points with certainty. Nevertheless, it was deduced that the natives are affable and not suspicious and are honest, except when some article catches their attention as being new and useful; and that they are polygamous, though, again, the short stay did not offer sufficient time for full investigation on this point.

The native houses are square, subterranean huts, well-constructed of thick planks, with roofs which touch the ground and circular entrances barely the width of a human body. The floor is very flat and clean and in the middle there is a square hole, one *vara* deep, for making and keeping a fire, which heats the entire inside of the house. Lastly, the construction of the houses is sturdy enough to protect the inhabitants from predatory animals.

In cold weather the men cover themselves with skins of deer, seal, sea otter, or the like; but if the temperature is tolerable they go about like true sons of Nature, except for wreaths of flowers[6] on their heads. All the men wear their hair long, sometimes in a knot, at other times loose over their shoulders, except for the children who wear it short.

Their ear lobes are pierced and in the hole they put a pin of very smooth and polished bone. They tie their waists and ankles with a thong or thread which they pull tight, and they also paint most of the body red or black. Their arms are tattooed with several bands[7] like those of our sailors who have figures or inscriptions on various parts of their bodies.

The women cover their heads with a well-woven cap[8] made of the fibers of some flexible trees or other plants, unknown to us, so tightly woven that water caught in them does not soak through. Their hair hangs in two braids between their ears and cheeks and is adorned by many flowers.[9] In place of ear-rings they wear the same pins as the men.[10] They also have their lower lips tattooed with three lines, two running down from the corners of the mouth to the point of the chin, the third from the middle of the upper part of the lip to the point of the chin. These tattoos are so distinct on the old women that there are scarcely any clear spaces between; the girls' faces, on the contrary, have such light lines that at a short distance they can scarcely be seen. Who knows whether this difference is the characteristic sign of age so that they show at first glance exactly how old they are?

Around their necks the women hang many necklaces of small fruit,[11] bone, and shells[12] which they gather on the beaches. They wear a sort of skin skirt, with a fringe of strings which hangs down to the calf. They protect themselves from the cold in the same way as the men, tying up their legs as far down as the foot.

The daily life of these people consists in observing the orders of a chief,[13] who divides them in groups to go out and search for their common sustenance both by sea and by land. They reunite at sunset, but after the people from both ships have retired, an Indian goes out to inspect the beach and the vicinity of the small town. The chief's rule does not extend to any individuals except those who compose this narrow society; and it was clearly observed that the chief's son commands the others when they are under arms, for then he covers his head with many feathers, which doubtless indicates his position. Who knows whether command by the chief's family is hereditary? Oh, how many facts have been lost because of lack of experience and sufficient knowledge for these investigations!

Many times the Indians asked help of the Spanish to defeat their enemies in the field. This is certain evidence of their wars with other neighboring towns although they were friendly with several Indian visitors who soon arrived at the beaches. They apparently number more than three hundred of all sexes and ages, divided into groups which doubtless form separate societies.[14] Among them was a year-old child who, with his little bow and arrow of a size suitable for his age, hit the palm of a hand raised as a target at a distance of two varas.[15]

Although care was taken in investigating their religion, no understanding of it was acquired, since we saw scarcely any superstitious manifestations except that one of the Indians spoke some words while turning successively to the four cardinal points of the compass, perhaps invoking the protection of some gods they considered rulers of the winds.

It was then discovered that one of them had died, and it appeared that after mourning him they burned the body inside the house of the captain, to which place they prevented the entrance of the Spanish. Once the house was entered, however, nothing noteworthy was found in it.[16]

As our stay was short, the pronunciation of their language could not be learned, and the lack of expression in the signs made did not permit mutual understanding, although the Indians did articulate readily many Spanish names.

Their offensive arms are arrows with flint points, flint knives, and some badly made knives of iron that appear to be pieces of old swords. According to their sign language, they had received these from more northerly places. One knife was seen with the mark (£), and on all knives they put handles of wood or bone through which they run a string to suspend it from the neck or from the wrist.

Of all the things that were given them nothing attracted their attention more than iron, whether in the rough or in the form of cutting arms.[17] Certainly this precious metal is the only one that would make them commit robbery or murder, or would spur them to superhuman efforts to obtain, since they consider it superior; and there is no doubt that, under the conditions in which they live, it offers them comfort and riches since it helps them build their frail vessels, and is of use in hunting and fishing. It is worth exposing themselves to the greatest danger to get it, in the same way that we risk our lives to extract silver and gold from the bowels of the earth; and certainly these metals are not, nor can they be, as useful as iron, if it were not for the arbitrary and conventional value given them.

The natives receive beads with appreciation, and tobacco pleases them greatly, for they cultivate it in small plots near their houses and smoke it in tubes similar to the mouthpiece of a trumpet.[18]

They do not enjoy our food and drink so much. Although they took it out of politeness, they threw it away when we were not looking. One of them became so familiar with the Spaniards that for several days he dressed in the clothes of his sailor friends; and to better accustom himself [to the foreign ways], he often sat down at the table in the presence of his countrymen. There he ate whatever he was given, a conformity which the Indians applauded, while the Spanish considered it a noble effort made by one who aspired to be called a cosmopolite.

They hunt deer, buffalo,[19] bear, seal, and sea otter (although the pursuit of the last two might be classed as fishing); they have never seen evidence of any other animals, nor were any others discovered on these shores.

The birds are crows, sparrow hawks, ducks, sea gulls, turtle doves, and very small birds; of these only a few of each were seen, perhaps because of the lack of fruit for food.

Fishing is for sardines, *pegerey, morcillones,* and *pies de cabra,* species which are abundant. We did not see them catch any other kinds from their canoes. This is doubtless because they lack equipment and hooks, or because necessity does not compel more difficult and laborious fishing. Consistent with the indolent situation in which Nature places them, they exert little more effort than that of Nature; hence there is less hostility toward their neighbors, fewer disputes about property, and less hate produced by ambition. Happy are they, if they continue for a long time in that peaceful state in which Mother Nature has placed them.

Several times efforts were made to find out whether foreign ships had previously arrived on these coasts, but the difficulty of understanding them made this attempt vain, except for the intelligence, conveyed by signs, that our party were the first to arrive in port in these lands. They readily explained that the old iron which some possessed came to them from more northerly lands by means of exchange. There is no doubt that the iron came from New Mexico by communication with some tribe or other, sometimes stable, sometimes nomadic, and that it circulated until it came into the hands of the inhabitants of the beach, who, because of their fishing, must be considered richer than many of the tribes and capable of paying for the precious material at prices sufficient to maintain the commerce.

Also we tried to find out if these people had any other metals, precious stones, or pearls, but there were no signs that would lead us to believe that they had knowledge of these. Even though many of them came to the beaches to trade their trifles and to receive beads to augment the necklaces they wore around their necks, nothing appeared in these ornaments except shells, particles of fish bones, and small periwinkles picked up from the beach.

The land asks only to be cultivated to produce in abundance the same fruits, more or less, as the countries of Europe. Its mountains are covered with tall pines which form a thick forest centuries old; its residue continually improves the soil, which supports fragrant green growth. It enchants the senses, for the mixture of rose, wild marjoram, lily, plantain, celery, thistle, camomile, and an infinite number of other plants that would be precious finds for a botanist are produced with that inconsistent disorder with which Nature knows how to divert the eyes of the observer and forms the most pleasing and agreeable garden imaginable.

Without any great exploration, since neither the shortness of the time nor the need for security permitted us to go very far from the beaches, we found strawberries, mulberries of both kinds, blackberries, sweet onions, and mushrooms, which we ate with pleasure in that happy paradise. These fruits were found most abundantly near the streams, which are frequent and crystal clear.

The pines are of extraordinary height; among those which we found fallen on the beaches and lacking their upper ends were some which measured sixty varas in length and two in diameter at the bottom.[20] This wood is good for decking, beams, and masts. It is very straight-grained, so the natives divide these large trunks into thick planks, since a wedge will split them straight to the opposite end.

The impossibility of penetrating the interior prevents our reporting on the form and variety of timber; for this reason, too, we saw no trees sufficiently large for the construction of vessels, although on the banks of the river there was evidence that there probably were such trees.

The map of the port was drawn with the greatest precision, and the harbor was sounded with accuracy. Its latitude was observed repeatedly at 41°07′ and its longitude was estimated at 19°04′ W. of San Blas.[21]

The western point of the port is a high head, which forms a peninsula into the sea and serves as protection from the winds of the fourth quadrant and even of part of the third. This peninsula is joined to the mainland by a hill, much lower and so narrow that at the neck there is scarcely room on its top for a narrow path leading to the peninsula. The port is thus protected from the winds of the first and second quadrant, remaining open only to those of the third, and there is no doubt that when they blow from that direction, high seas are produced in the entire bay. At such times it would not be safe to remain anchored in it. However, such winds blow only in the winter months; for the rest of the year the northwest or almost north winds are constant.

At the entrance to the port there is a small, barren, and very white island[22] that makes it visible from a distance, and inside there are an infinite number of high rocks which shelter it and keep the sea tranquil between them and the land. The cove where anchor was dropped is perfect for careening, and any ship can come close enough to shore to put its gangway on land with only the precaution of covering the cables that lie close to the coast [a necessary measure] since there are many small stones likely to abrade them if this precaution is neglected.

The facility that the beach offers for taking on water made the task scarcely any bother to the crews, for many creeks of crystal clear water run to the seashore, where they obtained it without any effort. In the same way, they gathered wood, which they got from huge dry trees on the beach.

The tides being so important in navigation, we observed them while we stayed here. There were two ebbs and two flows in twenty-four and four-fifths hours, the difference between ebb tides being that one receded seven feet and the other five. This inequality made us continue our observations, and these further studies not only corroborated the first, but also showed that on the thirteenth, when the conjunction occurred, the tides were greater, the first receding nine feet and the second six feet, high tide having occurred that day at noon.

From the top of the head that forms the peninsula a large river, which empties into the sea from between two mountains, was seen at a distance of three fourths of a league to the south.[23] Desiring to investigate its banks and to acquaint themselves with the wanderings of its course the men visited it. When they arrived they found it to be ten varas wide and two deep in the middle, and navigable by any launch, provided one could get past the mouth, for there the river widens and its depth decreases until it is almost impassable.

They went along its shores for almost a league and saw turtle doves of good size; they heard nightingales and other birds they did not recognize. They saw logs of extraordinary length, which convinced them that when there were floods or when it was wintertime, the river would wash over a plain one-quarter league wide, which lies between the two mountains; in this plain there are many quagmires and arroyos which confirm this conjecture.

At the edge of the mountains considerable fruit was found, more abundant than that eaten at the port, especially the mulberries, which the men picked with their own hands from the big trees that bear them.

On the nineteenth all that had to be done had been finished and sail was set at 8 A.M. with light northwest winds, the only ones encountered during the stay in that port. The weather becoming calm at twelve noon they anchored a short distance from the outer island.

JOURNAL OF DON BRUNO DE HEZETA, COMMANDER OF THE EXPEDITION AND CAPTAIN OF THE SANTIAGO, AT TRINIDAD BAY, JUNE 9-19, 1775

NINTH DAY. Following the same course I continued exploring the coast. At one-thirty we sighted three canoes of Indians, who were earnestly trying to approach the ship. I shortened sail, and they arrived, all without clothing and with their hair disheveled. In a short time they had exchanged with the sailors the skin clothes, which they had carried hidden. They went off, and a little later they followed our course to the harbor, where I anchored shortly after the schooner at 3:30 P.M. I went to sound a closed port which a small peninsula formed and to which I determined to warp. This task was finished the following day at 10 A.M., the ship being anchored in four or three and one-half fathoms forward and four aft.

Tenth day. In the afternoon I went ashore with the officers and some armed men to find out whether the friendliness which the Indians showed the day before during the visit they made to the ship was as genuine as it had been when I went ashore with Don Juan Francisco de la Bodega y Quadra and Don Francisco Mourelle. At that time we expressed our kind regard by giving them various trinkets made of beads, some of which I received from his Majesty's account, whereas others Don Juan Francisco had on his own account for the same purpose. I noted that the natives were somewhat suspicious that afternoon, although they did not try to obstruct us.

"Diario de la navegacion que debe hacer con el Divino auxilio el Teniente de Navio Dn. Bruno de Hezeta en la Fragato de su mando Santiago, alia Nueva Galicia, y en conserva de la Goleta Sonora que esta a su orden y se dirijen a los Descubrimientos de las Costas Septentrionales de la California desde el Departamento de San Blas situado en la latitud de 21 grados y 30 minutos N. y longitud occidental de Paris 110 grados segun la carta de M. Bellin que es por la que se had dirigido." Archivo General de Indias, Audiencia de Mexico, legajo 19.

I returned aboard before dark, after my crew had mingled with the natives for some time.

Eleventh day. Today I determined to take possession, because it is the noble day of the Most Holy Trinity. At dawn I sent Don Cristobal de Revilla and some armed men to find the paths which cross from the mainland to the peninsula that forms this port and to make ready the chapel, where the first Mass was to be celebrated with the greatest ceremony possible. These arrangements for public worship were made with complete liberty, since the Indians of that vicinity never thought of hindering them, in spite of the fact that some people from the near-by rancherias accompanied the soldiers. Coming ashore with the commander of the *goleta,* the Fathers, officers, and armed men of both ships, I set up a cross on the shore and, forming an extended front, we performed the first adoration.[24] Then, in as orderly a fashion as the narrow trails permitted, we followed the path to the top of the hill where the chapel was made, and took possession with the most scrupulous formality, as enjoined by the instructions given me. Mass was celebrated and a sermon was preached by the Reverend Father Miguel de la Campa. This ceremony was solemnized with several volleys of gunfire. Each of us returned to his own ship which, with banners waving, saluted with three volleys of artillery and "Long live the King." When I went to the rancheria in the afternoon, I found the natives terrified, but as we gave them more presents, they cast off their fear. In unmistakable ways they demonstrated their desire to establish eternal friendship with us. I assured them of it as long as they upheld the cross that had been set up that morning, pointing out to them why this act was necessary. This they all promised to do.

Twelfth day. To procure wood and water I sent part of the crew with some armed men, who, however, remained idle because the friendship of the Indians rather aided the men in their task than necessitated their remaining on guard. Both wood and water are found in abundance on the beach nearest the anchorage, a gunshot distant from the ships.

Thirteenth day. Observed with scrupulous examination that the daytime tides during my stay in this port ebbed only three and one half Parisian feet. I secured the ship under my command in sufficient water, allowing six feet extra at low tide for the pitch of the ship. At 3 P.M. the rudder scraped, and withdrawing a little, I anchored in four fathoms aft. I continued provisioning the same as the day before. I cut a tree for topmasts for foretop sails, since I found the two that I had almost useless, taking advantage of the good wood that is abundant here until another such place can be found for the replacement of deficiencies of this kind, as well as for a supply of water.

Fourteenth day. I spent the day working on the masts, ballasting the ship, and providing myself with wood and water. At review that night the apprentice seamen, José Antonio Rodriquez and Pedro Lorenzo, were missing.

Fifteenth day. This morning I armed some men, and in their company I went to the rancheria to inquire the whereabouts of the deserters. The confusion of the Indians made me think them guilty, and I seized the captain of this village and one of another rancheria who was there at this time, both of whom came with little urging. Although still of the same mind, in a short time I agreed to put them ashore again and to give them presents, on the advice of Don Juan Francisco la Cuadra and the Reverend Fathers.

Sixteenth day. I went on with the same job of providing myself with wood, water, and ballast, this being the first stop which we made for these supplies. One of the deserters I mentioned yesterday, the apprentice, Pedro Lorenzo, returned. A declaration was taken from him. He said that the chief of that Indian rancheria had suggested that he stay with him and offered him dominion of all those lands with all their resources; that he had determined to remain, and that, guided by the Indians, who provided him with food, he had been conducted to a summit next to the anchorage where a lookout was maintained among the trees. But the guards accompanying him became careless, and, repenting his action, he fled. My first suspicion being thus confirmed, I crossed to the shore this afternoon with some men, thinking that at the first threats the natives would return the other missing deserter. They were terrified and made excuses in great confusion. I made the informer [i.e., Lorenzo] come, and in their presence he stated that the confession he had made this morning was false. By punishing this man on the spot, I satisfied the Indians, who for the rest of my stay continued to express their friendship.

Seventeenth day. I continued fitting out for departure, sparing no pains to hasten the preparation, and I sent the watch to draw the map geometrically.

Eighteenth day. Today, the map of the port, which had been made in collaboration with the captain of the *goleta,* Don Juan Francisco Bodega de la Quadra, and First Pilot Don Francisco Mourelle, was finished. I went with the latter to explore a river which had been named Tortolas,[25] and the adjacent fields and forests, and to make other observations. From the Indian inhabitants I received the greatest hospitality; and, wishing to recompense them, I brought most of them aboard in my launch to repay their good treatment with beads. I went to the near-by rancheria, where with melancholy faces they said goodbye. Giving them presents, I offered to return, which consoled them.

Although the labor of my command during my stay in the Port of Trinidad kept me busy, it did not prevent me from having some leisure to observe the customs of the Indians in this small village, as well as the Indians of the vicinity, who also frequently got together to visit us; and to observe the advantages that the country offers, both for agriculture and for a settlement, if that is considered. These Indians and their neighbors are of medium corpulence, robust and agile, without beauty in either sex; they are brown-skinned, with long shiny hair, black sparkling eyes, and with little facial hair. The men wear no clothes, not even to hide their genitals, and only when obliged to by the cold do they cover themselves with the well-tanned skins of deer, buffalo, antelope, bear, or sea otter and with a sort of woven skirt of rabbit and other flexible skins, which are soft enough to use without discomfort.

The women cover themselves from the waist to the knees with a skirt of dressed skin or of grass, some ending in a sort of fringe, with fringe at top and bottom. Thus with careful handiwork, they voluntarily preserve their modesty. Interested, like their sex every-

Discovery and Exploration

where, in ornament, they like beads; but they have no great appreciation of flannel and woolens.

On certain days the captains and their sons wear on their heads a garland, made of fine skins, grasses, or feathers, which distinguishes them from the others.

These Indians are affable, docile, and timid—they love, respect, and obey the eldest, who governs with his council; according to my understanding, each rancheria is made up only of his descendants. When old age makes a captain useless for war, the best-fitted son becomes captain.

Lack of communication prevented my asking about their knowledge of minerals. But two members of the crew who were thought intelligent were given this job and informed me that in the small area they explored they had seen nothing which might promise such resources.

Iron is the metal that the natives particularly esteem, because they know its advantage for the arms they use are the arrow, lance, knife, or dagger, whose points or edges are of well-worked flint. They also use iron knives, which they generally carry dangling from their necks by a cord and which, when they lack confidence in dealing [with strangers] they hold grasped in the hand.

With great curiosity, I inquired several times whence came the iron knives or with whom they had bartered for them. They all answered by pointing to the coast to the north, except one who, with vivid and intelligent signs, conveyed to us that his had been made from a spike from the wreckage of a ship which the sea had cast up onto the beach.

When they go to war or to treat with their enemies, they paint the face or body black or with colors, doubtless believing that it makes them more horrible and terrifying.

They all asserted that they had not seen any ships on these seas, but that they had news that ships frequented those coasts, pointing to the south; and I am of the opinion these are the ships that come to Monterey.

These Indians have a well-ordered economy, hunting wild animals and fishing for shellfish or other fish, with which activities they sustain themselves collectively. They leave to the women the gathering of wild seeds, fragrant plants, and small fruits which also serve them as sustenance; and they sow only tobacco which, even without being cured, is not bad tasting.

Their dwellings are small houses made of boards, with small oval doors, built so as to be sheltered from winds of the fourth quadrant, which are the coldest and most prevalent.[26]

They also have other houses which are subterranean, and in the center of these they keep a fire burning, where they offer their sacrifices. And, though this I do not state positively, here they burn their dead and here the oldest people live.[27]

The greatest diligence has not enabled me to learn what sect they belong to or what type of paganism they adhere to. I only know that the practice of polygamy is prevalent.[28]

All of the coasts, mountains, and fields I examined during my stay at the Port of Trinidad are covered with a luxuriant growth. Thick, tall, straight pines of the best quality for curved decking and for masts, intermixed with middling good white poplar, extend inland from the shore itself, leaving little room for cultivation.

Both in these woods and in the small meadows there is such luxuriant pasturage that I believe it could maintain an infinite amount of livestock without difficulty. The plants I could recognize are wild marjoram, celery, peppermint, camomile, verbena, lilies, and roses of Castile. Among the trees are mulberry trees that bear both yellow fruit and violet fruit, as in Spain. They taste less sweet than those of Spain.

The temperature is colder than that of Europe in the same latitude; this I suspect is due to the thick, humid fogs which frequently fill the atmosphere. In my opinion the abundance of springs of water is a result of this same phenomenon. These springs are found everywhere, for in one hundred and eighty *tuesas*[29] that I measured on the beach as a base for the map I drew, I counted six springs, three of which were sufficient to replace my water supply. They were crystal clear.

The river[30] is not very full. At this season its water is mixed with sea water for a distance of three fourths of a league from its mouth,

Discovery and Exploration

which is as far as I went. It is about six tuesas deep. Inland its depth is sufficient to flat the largest launch or the heaviest tree trunk one might wish to convey from the near-by mountains; only at its mouth is it necessary to await high tide in order to enter or leave.

Several trees of great size, found lying on the fields next to the river, indicate that during floods its waters extend about a half or three fourths of a league on either side, and inundate the near-by plains, which appeared to me to be most fertile.

The port is closed, though on the map it does not look so because the map does not extend to the sea. The coast goes from the end I called *"cañada"* to a cape which I named "Punta Gorda," NNE and SSW and following on a line in that direction; which will convince anyone of its safety.

Ships ought to remain moored at a distance of eight to ten fathoms from shore in the area within a line from the mountain with the cross,[31] and be secured with an anchor to the SE, a cable fastened to shore to the SW, and two stern moorings from the poop, one to the NE and the other to the N and both to land, with the precaution that the poop remain in five and a half fathoms of water at high tide. In this way one could avoid having the SW cable suffer any abrasion, for the bottom here is clear, but the area farther in is full of rocks. If I had known this in advance, I would have saved the loss of a cable which I ruined, in spite of having it buoyed.

Fishing for small shell fish is good, but I have not seen any other fish, except some sardines[32] dried without salt, which the Indians gave us in barter and which I did not disdain. We had no fresh meat left except for the sick, and those of us in the cabin were living on rations of jerked beef.

I attribute this scarcity of sea food to its not being the right season; the few fish available at this time are hard to catch or are eaten by the many seals and sea otter.

The tides in all phases of the moon are like those of the ocean. They have two flows and ebbs in twenty-four and a fifth hours. At the opposition or full of the moon this rise and fall is greater, much the same as on the Cantabrian coast. I was not able to verify whether this happened during an eclipse, because I left before that happened.

The tides differ from those of Europe only in the fact that the two which occur in twenty-four and four-fifths hours are not equal, one rising little more than half the other, so that during regular tides the greater rose six to seven Parisian feet, the other four to four and a half. In the waning of the moon the highest tide attains ten feet, the other five or six.

Landfalls are easily made on these exposed coasts, although the calculation of the longitude may be greatly in error unless one is warned that about one hundred or more leagues before approaching it [the port] one encounters what in European waters they call *aguas malas,* and here are *caravelas,* rhomb-shaped waves, with a crest like a lateen sail. From seventy leagues out other waves, called *porras,* are met. Their shape is like a white squash, with the sole difference that the neck extends from ten to twelve feet on some and the head is smaller in comparison with the caravelas. Closer to land the sea gradually loses color and becomes more turbulent, so that near the coast one finds a mixture of earth with plants and floating roots woven together that they call "balsas."

It is not only these signs which give certain indication of the nearness of the coast; birds, which they call "centenares," are also evident at a distance of forty leagues from shore, whereas others with a form like that of a parrot, with black body and red legs and head, can be seen at a distance of five or six leagues.

A settlement in this Port of Trinidad, besides its suitability as it appears to me, for the extension of the Gospel (the first object of our Sovereign), is also necessary not only to assure the protection it offers to ships of medium size, but also because it would be difficult to dislodge any foreigner who might take possession of it. It has an inviting location for the establishment of a colony, from which it would be easy to penetrate into the interior of the land, a circumstance which would result in known detriment to the Royal Treasury.

All of the headland with the cross on it that I show on the map has a steep slope, and its elevation dominates all the level country. This, with several springs of water that I saw running down to the sea from the headland, would make it impregnable if a cut were made in the narrow pass communicating with the mainland, where the land declines at a forty-five degree angle. This itself would greatly facilitate the construction I suggest.

If the garrison did not exceed sixty men, there would be enough land for sown crops and for raising livestock, so that without any other aid the men could live comfortably without leaving the limits of the fortification, where the quality of the black soil is apparently easy to work.

Nineteenth day. I left this port...."

DIARY OF FRAY MIGUEL DE LA CAMPA, CHAPLAIN OF THE SANTIAGO, AT TRINIDAD BAY, JUNE 9–19, 1775

NINTH DAY.—At 2 p.m. four canoes, with twenty-four Indians, overtook us. Having come somewhat near they stopped, but upon our making signs for them to draw nearer they did so without any misgiving. They received sea biscuits and other things which we gave them to eat, and they bartered some sea-otter skins and deerskins with the sailors for knives, and with great pleasure said good-by, raising their hands. The schooner which went ahead gave the signal of a port and good anchorage, and following in the frigate, we anchored in seven fathoms, at 4 p.m. We observed that two of the canoes that were following us went over to the schooner, and the Indians went aboard. Then they came to the frigate and brought the captain of the schooner in their canoe. They came aboard and were given beads, which they valued greatly, and they went ashore to a rancheria opposite us.

Tenth day. On the tenth the ship was made secure. Because of the report that our first visitors gave to the Indians of the rancheria of the port, not only the men but also the women came. All had crowns of flowers. They accepted what was given them without hesitation. We gave them to understand that we wished to go to their rancheria, which they permitted. In the afternoon we went ashore. They came out to meet us but with some misgiving. Some came armed, but their captain ordered them to unstring their bows. We entered their houses, where their occupations and their poverty were evident. One of them brought a little camomile and offered it to a sailor, and when he took it, the Indian asked a knife in exchange; but the sailor did not think it well to exchange the knife so cheaply, and gave him back his plant. The only thing in which they showed a lack of interest was clothing, for the Commandant

---

"Diario del viaje qu hice a bordo de la Fragata del Rey Nombrada Santiago desde el Puerto de S^n Blas al nuevo descubrim^{to} por la costa de Monterrey hta. el grado 50." Archivo General de Indias, Audiencia de Mexico, legajo 104-6-17.

gave the captain a jacket and some kerchiefs, which, after being accepted, were returned; but he [the commandant] made a sign that they keep them. Their houses are few, not more than seven; they are made of boards and have oval doors, which are very low and appear more to be kennel holes. They close them with a sliding board, and so we did not see what they were like inside. Two of the Indians had small enclosures where a little tobacco was growing, since they are fond of smoking a pipe. The men go about completely naked, wearing only some chamois-colored deerskins, with the fur turned inside for better protection, to shield themselves from the cold. The women cover themselves in the same way; in addition, in back they have a sort of skirt of the same material, which they try to adorn with palm-shaped embroidery, and at the bottom they leave many very thin strings like a fringe. In front they have skirts of reed grass. The women also have their chins tattooed with three black stripes, which disfigure them greatly. The men draw various designs on their arms. Everyone wears his hair long, except the boys and girls who wear it cut short, those who are not married being thus distinguished. They have two or three wives; (but) we did not see that they had any special one. Their arms are bows and arrows, some flint lances, and some flints four to six *dedos*[33] long in the form of pikes set in some short wooden handles. They also have some pieces of swords about a palm in length which, by means of signs, they told us came from the north. Asked if they acquired any from elsewhere they said no, only to the north, and that there were larger ones there. Only one of them gave us to understand by means of very expressive signs that his had been made from a spike which he took from a piece of wood that washed ashore, and which he had pounded out by blows with stones.

Eleventh day. On the eleventh of this year our Holy Mother Church celebrates the ineffable mystery of the Most Blessed Trinity, and in honor of this sovereign mystery Commandant Don Bruno de Hezeta determined to take possession of this land in the name of our Catholic Majesty. To make ready for this ceremony, at dawn he sent Don Cristobal Revilla with some armed men to make, on the summit of the hill which shelters port, a bower adorned with the greatest care for celebrating the Holy Sacrifice of the Mass. Having been notified that we could come up, we went ashore with all the officers, and the greater part of the men of the frigate and of the schooner. After landing we all worshipped the Holy Cross that had been made to be placed at the top of the mountain. My companion, Fray Benito de la Sierra, and I sang "Te Deum Laudamus"; then, with the men going in good order, we ascended, but not without difficulty because of the rough, steep, and somewhat dangerous path. Having arrived at the summit, we set up the Holy Cross,[34] and the commandant took possession with all the formality prescribed in the instructions of Antonio Maria Bucareli. This act completed, I said Mass and preached amid great quiet and calmness, for the Indians were content to observe what we were doing from the rancheria. The event of the day was the motive for giving the Port the name of the Most Holy Trinity. From the top of this mountain we saw a river, which cannot be seen from the port; it enters the sea to the east of the port. Afterwards it was named the Rio de las Tortolas.

On descending we met four Indians near the beach, and to the one whom the afternoon before we had judged most intelligent, the captain of the schooner said to say "Long live Charles III," and he, very happily, repeated along with our men "Long live Charles III." He was not astonished by the thunder of the artillery, which in turn answered the salutes that the men on shore fired with their muskets. Those in the rancheria did not enjoy it much, because the noise of the cannon and the strength of the echo resounding among the mountains made them tremble with fear, as they themselves told us when we went to visit them in the afternoon. By signs it was explained to them what happened, and they were made to understand that they were our friends. The cross was pointed out to them, and they were charged not to take it down. Their captain made a long speech to them, and they promised that they would not take it down.[35]

Twelfth day. On the twelfth we began taking on provisions of water and wood. The commandant sent a guard for any eventuality that might occur, but there was no necessity for this precaution, because the Indians were so friendly that they aided us in our work. We went ashore to eat, and as we were seated, many Indians came from the rancheria by the river with their wives and children. They came among us, and one sat down next to me. They received what was given them in the way of beads; and they tasted what we gave them from the table and kept it. But when a plate of mussels was put on the table, they could not contain themselves, but put their hands into the plate, especially the Indian next to me, who ate with great pleasure. He smiled and embraced me many times. The meal ended, and they all went away pleased.

Thirteenth day. On the thirteenth the frigate touched bottom, for the tide was lower than on the other days, since on this day there was full moon. Today was spent in securing the ship.

Fourteenth day. On the fourteenth we continued to take on wood and water; we found both on the same beach, for to its shores flow many streams of very good water. I counted as many as seven. The two that are the most plentiful flow from the near-by hills, and between these two the Indians have their rancheria at the foot of a hill.... shelters them from the northwest wind—the prevailing wind on this coast. Some sailors went to the Indians' houses and saw them busily occupied in one house, which was underground and well sheltered; the floor was covered with boards, and in the center there was a fair-sized pit made of stones, in which they always kept a fire. It was observed that they went in, and by mourning indicated that they felt some grief. They came out sweating very much and they then washed themselves; then, entering, they continued their weeping. They explained that someone had died and they were burning him, which was evident from the bad odor from the underground house.

Many people came to visit us from the two rancherias nearest the port, which are the largest.[36] In the afternoon we went ashore to see the guests and give them presents. I asked them if any other ships had arrived there. They answered no, but that farther down, pointing in the direction of Monterey, they knew that large ships came. I gave them to understand that indeed two came every year; that we were they who were there; and that little by little we would advance toward them. They were greatly pleased, especially a big boy who embraced me, laughing very happily. Another asked us by means of a very clear sign, if we were men like himself. I believe his curiosity was born of the little regard that our men showed for their women, as they faithfully observed the prudent orders which the commandant had issued. That night two sailors were missing.[87]

Fifteenth day. Today, the fifteenth, the festival of Corpus Christi was celebrated. A holiday was observed and the men rested.

Sixteenth day. On the sixteenth one of the deserters, compelled by hunger, returned in the launch that went to carry the men to work. By his lies he confirmed the commandant's suspicion that the Indians were accomplices in the desertion. For the deserter said that they had invited him to stay, and had hidden him, and had made him other offers. Thereupon the captain determined to accuse the Indians and oblige them to turn over the other [deserter]; and it was decided that the one deserter would be taken along, so that the accusation could be made in his presence. The Indians proved their innocence, explaining that, far from hiding him, they had rather warned us by shouting that he was fleeing. Thereupon, in front of them, the deserter was given a scourging with gun straps. They would have scourged him to the skin, had not the Indians interceded, imploring mercy on his behalf.

Eighteenth day. On the eighteenth the commandant went with the pilot of the schooner to explore the Rio de las Tortolas; they found that the water is somewhat salty for a half league distant and that at this season the amount of water in the river not great. But it was evident that in the wet season the stream is large, for its bed is more than a half league wide. They saw some poplars and many mulberry trees. The Indians gave us dried sardines, and some came aboard with the captain in the launch and were recompensed with beads. During our stay in this port the Indians behaved with friendship and confidence, for they entered our launches with us to come aboard and took our people in their canoes. These canoes are not very long, being at most little more than four varas in length, but they are well made with two bows.[89] Generally, they are in one piece and very solid. The natives could make them longer, since there are pines [redwood] with which to do it. In the river a very thick tree trunk was found, so long that, consumed by curiosity, we measured it and found it to be forty-seven varas long. But the Indians are content with what they need for fishing for the mussels which are plentiful, and which are their regular food. I did not see any other fish in this port, or along the adjacent coast which we explored. We saw only some dried sardines, which the Indians brought to trade for beads. Seals, which the Indians also eat, are abundant, and the Indians have in their houses a supply of meat and many bladders full of the fat of these animals. They preserve many pieces in the manner of ham; they heat these over the fire, and catch the fat on some pounded plants, which they eat with great pleasure. Also some sea otters are seen, but they are not so abundant as the seals.

The port is situated in 41° 6' of latitude and is well protected, but the greater part of it has a rocky bottom. Because of lack of experience we let out an anchor chain here, which, having been in the water only three days, emerged in very bad condition. The hill that shelters the port is really a peninsula, since it is attached to the land only at the north. It dominates the whole port, and is suitable for a fort, since the part that looks out to sea is covered with rocks. At the south end a trickle of water runs down to the sea. According to our observations the climate is cold, and it is commonly cloudy. During the short time that the sun was out, we went out to enjoy it as if it were winter. The land is humid and very fertile, for the trees come down to the very beach. Here we saw an abundance of strawberries. The hills are covered with thick, tall, straight pines. The land is full of grass and there are many plants and flowers—roses of Castile, lilies, camomile, mint, celery, pennyroyal, marjoram, verbena, and other fragrant plants which the Indians eat. They also gave us yellow mulberries and purple ones; the latter are better tasting than the yellow. Of birds I saw only crows, sparrow hawks, and sparrows; but those who went to the river said that they had seen doves, nightingales, and others that they did not know. Of animals, judging by the skins seen among the Indians, deer abound, and there are plenty of bear; and there are apparently also buffalo

[elk], since a skin was seen among the Indians and we even saw tracks on the banks of the river. When we went to say good-by to the Indians, they showed by the expression of their faces the sorrow they felt at our departure, and by signs they told us that they would mourn five days. Without our telling them anything about the cross, they said on their own account that they would not take it down and that they would take care that no one else took it down, and that whenever we returned we would find it there.

Nineteenth day. The nineteenth we set sail.

JOURNAL OF DON FRANCISCO ANTONIO MOURELLE, SECOND PILOT OF THE SONORA, AT TRINIDAD BAY, JUNE, 1775

While we were dallying in entering port, we saw two canoes leave the north shore and approach the frigate, and the natives began to trade their pelts for beads[40] and other trifles, which the sailors exchanged with them. Also, while dropping anchor, we observed a small rancheria at the edge of a mountain within the port, but no canoes came out from it.

Having finished our tasks, we went to sound the innermost part of the port and, finding sufficient depth to anchor a stone's throw from the beach, we warped the *goleta* until we penetrated the main part of the port. We let out two cables to land and made them fast on some rocks which Nature provided for the purpose; we also let go two anchors, one to the southeast and the other to the southwest, which precaution the frigate also took.

As soon as we had anchored, some Indians from canoes came aboard our ship and without the least misgiving mixed with our men, exchanging their pelts for the beads that were given them.

Although the French chart [of Bellin] marks this landfall, conspicuously, considering the obvious errors of the chart both in the location of the capes and in the representation of the coast, it seems likely that the inaccuracy in its construction is the cause of the vague supposition of some large bays, which we found neither to the north

---

"Navegacion hecha por el Piloto segundo de la Armada Don Franco. Antonio Maurelle en la Goleta de S. M. nombrada la Sonora del mando del Tenienta de Fragata Don Juan Francisco de la Bodega y Cuadra, a los descubrimientos de las Costas, y mares Septentrionales de la California, que por orden del Excelentisimo Senor Bo. Frey Don Antonio Maria de Bucarely y Ursua, egecutaron el ano de 1775." Archivo General de Indias, legajo 19.

The most accessible and oft-used version of Mourelle's account is that contained in Daines Barrington's *Miscellanies* (London, 1781), pp. 471*–534*. Where discrepancies exist between the 1781 translation and ours they are indicated in the notes. The letter B. indicates the Barrington translation.

nor to the south. By it [the chart], it is certain that we should be at Cape Fortuna, which it puts eight or ten leagues south of Cape Mendocino, but we are actually twenty leagues north of the latter, an error of two degrees in latitude for these capes.

On the eleventh we finished the work of anchoring and decided to take possession on a high mountain which forms the entrance to the port. To this end some of the men were divided into various detachments to be posted in the necessary places so the rest could march in an orderly fashion without danger of any attack. Advance sentinels were also posted at a distance to discover the paths along which the Indians go. Having taken over the roads at the most defensible places, the men marched in two armed bodies, having adored the holy cross [on the beach] at the time of disembarking. Arriving at the top of the mountain, they formed a square, in the center of which was the chapel. The cross was presented, Mass was celebrated with a sermon, and possession was taken with all the ceremony which our instructions directed. The occasion was celebrated with several artillery and cannon salvos, a noise which made the Indians tremble and frightened them, they believing that we had some unconquerable forces. But learning that no harm would result from our ceremony, they gathered to pay us a visit and perhaps to inquire about the unseen disturbance which had so astonished them.

Since the day of taking possession fell on the day that our mother Church celebrates the Most Holy Trinity, that name was given to the port.

On the succeeding days we began to take on wood and water, and we boot-topped in order to clean the bottom of the ship.⁴¹ We also made topmasks and yards to add main topsails, to see if with these we might make better sailing time.

We were also careful in observing the Indians, their way of life, habitations, clothing, diet, dominion, religious rites, language, their use of arms, the things they like best, their hunting and fishing. Although our distrust of a barbaric people made us attentively observe their customs, yet we never noted any actions on their part suggesting anything but the most loyal friendship and the fullest confidence in our men, by whom, in turn, they were treated with kindness and sociability.

Their houses were some square huts, strongly constructed of heavy boards, whose roofs touch the ground. For doors they have some circular holes, only large enough for a man's body to slip through.

The floor is perfectly level and very clean with a square pit in the center a vara deep; in this they make and keep a fire, beside which they warm themselves from the continual cold; and in this house finally, they are protected from wind and animals all the time they are asleep.

The men wear no clothes except when it is too cold, and then they put pelts of seal, sea otter, deer, or other animals over their shoulders, and on the head many put only a crown of fragrant plants. They wear their hair long, hanging over their shoulders or in a bundle (*en castaña*). The children were the only ones seen with short hair. In the lobes of their ears they wear two screws,[42] like the screw pin of a gun. They tie the waist and leg near the ankle strongly with a leather strap or a string. The face and the greater part of the body is regularly painted black or yellow.[43]

They have their arms tattooed with various bands, which they display, much as the common people in Spain often have ships and anchors tattooed on them.

The women cover their heads with a crown of willow that in the Kingdom they call a *corita,* and they wear their hair in two tresses, interspersed with various fragrant plants, hanging over their cheeks.

They wear the same kind of bone screws in their ears that the men do; they cover their bodies with the same kinds of pelts, and also for decency they wear a sort of skin skirt a half vara long with some threads forming a fringe. Their legs are tied tightly like the men's.

Their lower lips are tattooed in three stripes, of which two come from the corners of the mouth to the point of the chin, the other similarly from the upper middle part of the lower lip to the point of the chin, leaving some clear places, which we observed were much larger on the girls than on the old women; among the latter the chin is almost covered with tattooing. This imperfection totally disfigures their faces. Around the neck they wear some necklaces made of various fruits or of bone; others are made of small shells, which they pick up on the seashore.

The daily life of these people consists in observing the orders of a captain, who directs some of the people to go to sea and others to go inland to seek the necessary sustenance for all. In this way, he ordered one of them to search the beach at the time of our departure, which was at dusk. Nevertheless all of them were gathered together at sunset.

His domain appears to extend only to his town or rancheria, and the near-by mountains and beaches. They carry on war with other sections, and they asked aid against these enemies, making signs that they would be happy to take us along to subjugate them. Nevertheless there were several friendly rancherias, for more than three hundred Indians assembled in several groups with their women and children. It is evident that they did not permit some of these groups to enter the area around their houses.

At this time we saw a child, who could hardly have been one year old, shooting arrows with a bow in proportion to his strength and height; he would hit a hand at a distance of two or three yards, if they offered it as a target.

Since we had not seen any idols among them, even any sacrifices, we tried to ask them some questions which would give us information about this, and an investigation was casually made of how many wives each had. We found out without doubt they had a plurality of wives; from this we inferred with some justification that they are perfect atheists, in spite of the fact that, as we believe, they mourn for a dead Indian and cremate him inside the house of the chief. But we cannot for this reason assume any idolatry in them, because the mourning may be the effect of sentiment and the cremation may be based on pity and on the desire not to make the dead food for wild beasts, or it is perhaps a convenient way of avoiding the stench which the body would occasion.

We are left in doubt about the opinion we formed of their customs; they allowed us in their houses, except for that of the captain, but even when we overcame this difficulty [and entered the captain's house], we found nothing in it different from others.

It was not possible to understand the language. In spite of our efforts to understand them, signs had to be used all the time, and occasionally both parties remained in equal ignorance. Nevertheless they pronounce our words easily.

Their defensive arms are generally arrows with flint points, knives of flint, and some of iron, which appear to be pieces of old sabres. It was understood that they got these arms farther north, and among them we saw some knives with handles of wood or bone with the mark (£)," which they carry hanging on a string from the wrist or from the neck.

They place great stock in iron, greatly valuing knives, old cask hoops, and any other worthless little thing. They readily accepted beads and scorn clothing and food. Though they civilly took bread, meat, and other food, they pretended to try it, but really threw it away, though a little before our departure they kept the hardtack and it appeared to us that they ate it. Among them was one who exhibited the greatest confidence with us, and he sat down at the table and ate in the presence of his fellow countrymen.

They smoke tobacco in wooden pipes like a small trumpet, and we observed some little gardens where they had it planted.

The game with which they provide themselves is deer, buffalo [elk], seal, and sea otter, but we saw no indication of any others. Nor did we find any other birds along the sea shore except crow-like birds of prey, small birds, sea ducks, seagulls, and some black birds similar to parrots both in [the shape of] the head and in their flight, and with flesh-colored feet, breasts, and bills.

Fishing is restricted to sardines, pegerey, and morcillones and they take home only what is necessary for their daily food.

We tried to find out whether other people had traded with them or if they had seen any other ships but we tried in vain, for they were never able to understand us. Nonetheless we inferred that no other ships had arrived at this port.

We also tried to find out whether they had any metals and precious stones; but in addition to finding nothing among them which would verify this point or even leave it in doubt, we ascertained that they knew nothing of the things we showed them in an effort to make them understand what we were attempting to discover.

As much of the land as we have seen leaves us in no doubt as to its fertility, as we believe it capable of producing whatever is grown in Europe. Cold, clear water flows from all its deep arroyos and it is covered with wild plants like the European meadows. It has a verdure and aroma which makes it agreeable to sight and smell, and in it grow roses of Castile, wild marjoram, lilies, plantain, celery, thistles, camomile, and infinite others common to the country.

We also saw strawberries, mulberries, blackberries, sweet onions, and mushrooms, all in considerable abundance, particularly in the vicinity of the rivers. Among the plants we observed one similar to parsley (although odorless), which the Indians gather; they pound it and mix it with buffalo [elk] grease and eat it.

The mountains are covered with a thick, tall, straight type of pine tree, among which some seventy varas long and more than two varas in diameter at the base were measured. All the trees of this type are suitable for masts, decking and beams.

The outline of the port was geometrically drawn up by the Teniente de Navio and Commandante de la Goleta, Don Juan Francisco de la Bodega y Quadra, and by myself [map 1]. Although the plate represents the port as excessively open, it has to be imagined that the coast extends farther on to shelter the port, so that it is in the long run well protected from the southwest, west, northwest, north, northeast, and east winds. This was discovered on June ninth, the day we entered, by the commandant of the *goleta,* by sounding to the innermost part of the port.

On the western end of the port there is a mountain fifty tuesas high, connected at the north with the mainland where there is another eminence of twenty tuezas, and these provide not only sufficient protection from the wind, but also from any enemy. At the entrance is a rather high island[15] without any vegetation, and along the shores of the coast are many high rocks which by their shelter provide a perfect landing place.

Ships can anchor so close to the mountain that it may be practicable to put a ladder to shore. Only near the sandy beach are there

Discovery and Exploration

small rocks that make it necessary to cover the cables to the southeast and southwest. Nevertheless, if you anchor farther out it will not be necessary to do this.

We took aboard all our water from the beach, where many streams empty, and without much trouble we also gathered wood.

We paid no little attention to the tides, and we saw that they had the same characteristics as in Europe, taking six and a quarter hours for each flood and ebb, except that we noted that one of these ebbed six feet and the other only five. This inequality prompted us to repeated experiments, and not only did these substantiate the first observations, but also on the thirteenth, which was the conjunction of the moon, the tides were greater, just as in Spain. On this day the first tide ebbed nine feet, the other six; it was also found that high tide occurred at twelve o'clock on this day.

By repeated observations we tried to ascertain the latitude of the port, and always found it to be 41°7′ North, and we estimated it at 19°4′ West of San Blas.

There was now nothing left for us to discover from the reconnaissance of the port except to investigate a river flowing toward us from the southeast, which was discovered from the top of the mountain. We therefore went to see it in the launch on the eighteenth. We found that its mouth was wider than necessary for an outlet, and because of this the water spread out over a sand bar in such a way that we could not enter with the boat, and to do this we had to await high tide. Nevertheless, we disembarked on its banks and proceeded over a plain for a distance of a league. We found that the river was everywhere about ten varas wide and about two and a half varas deep in the middle.

Along its banks were strewn trees of greater girth and length than we had seen on the coast. This evidence showed us that in time of floods a plain of a quarter of a league or more is inundated, an opinion verified by several tule beds and arroyos, which there are all around.

We named this river the Tortolas, because when landing we saw some good-sized *tortolas* as well as other birds that we knew; among them some that had a very sweet song.

On the slopes of the mountains we found the same fruits as at the Port of Trinidad, although in greater abundance. Thus we concluded our intended investigation of this section of the coast.

On the eighteenth of June at 8 A.M. we hoisted anchor."

DIARY OF DON JUAN PEREZ, SECOND IN COMMAND OF THE SANTIAGO, AT TRINIDAD BAY, JUNE, 1775

TENTH DAY *to Sunday the Eleventh of June, 1775.* Night fell and the day dawned, clouded over with extremely cold and damp fog; nevertheless the two captains dressed themselves in their uniforms and at four o'clock we went ashore with forty armed men. The Indians apparently received us very coldly and with a certain lack of confidence, as is very natural on seeing numbers of unknown men. At six o'clock we returned aboard, having had no trouble. Tonight we prepared everything necessary in order to take possession the following day, which was done on the morning of the eleventh of June, the day of the Most Holy Trinity, with all of that formality that the Viceroy had ordered in his instructions or formulary. This ceremony was held at twelve noon atop the round hill that shelters the port.

Eleventh Day to Monday the Twelfth of June, 1775. Tonight at 2 A.M. we felt several blows on the bottom received by our keel owing to low water. It was necessary to slack off on the cables with which we were moored aft, and the anchor that we had to the east was hoisted. Hauling in the cable, we found it frayed in several places by the rocks that are very abundant on the bottom.

Twelfth Day to Tuesday the Thirteenth of June, 1775. The majority of these twenty-four hours were spent in finishing the mooring of the ship. I took a bearing on the limits of the port; its entrance and exit bear by the compass NNW 5°W [332 1/2°] and SSE 5°E [152 1/2°]; the small barren island forming the mouth of the inlet bears ESE 5°S [117 1/2°] a cable's length [120 fathoms] distant; the round hill on which the cross was erected bears S 8°SE [172°], a half cable's length [60 fathoms] distant; and the end of the coast that is seen in the distance bears S 1/4 SE, distant eight leagues, a little more or less.

Archivo General y Publica de la Nacion, Historia, Vol. 324.

Thirteenth Day to Wednesday the Fourteenth of June, 1775. This morning the captain ordered most of the crew ashore to collect water and gather wood, as was very proper, the men returning aboard in the afternoon. It was not noted that two sailors were missing until the morning of the fifteenth at eight o'clock, at which time the captain was informed. When he heard the news the color left his face but soon returned, and he paced to and fro in great anger. Ordering that ten men arm themselves with guns, pistols, and sabres, he went off ashore with them. Disembarking on the beach they met two poor old Indians, and the captain asked them what they had done with his two sailors. The poor devils, seeing his anger directed toward them, without their understanding or knowing the motive, began to tremble from pure fright. On seeing this the captain ordered those with him to put the Indians in the launch in order to bring them aboard; and according to the reports of what he said in the presence of many people, he declared he would give each of them two hundred lashes and that he would not set them free until the two sailor deserters should appear. Finally the men brought them aboard with the intention of carrying out the punishment the captain was determined to give them, [and this would have been done], if it had not been for the protest of his officers and those of the schooner. The captain saw that no one encouraged him in his purpose, but that on the contrary, [many were of the opinion] that the Indians should be given presents and should be taken ashore, without our letting them know anything of what had been intended; and this was done.

Fourteenth Day to Thursday the Fifteenth of June, 1775. The crew spent these twenty-four hours collecting water and gathering both wood and ballast. The names of the two deserters are Jose Antonio Rodriquez and Pedro Lorenzo. This very day the captain sent twelve armed men in search of the deserters. On arriving ashore the men were to go to the rancheria by the most direct route and search fully all of the houses or huts of the Indians, but the search was without results.

Fifteenth Day to Friday the Sixteenth of June, 1775. The search was conducted in such a way that the Indians were astonished at what was done to their houses, without knowing the motive or purpose. This turn of events was sufficient to make them change the good opinion they had formed of us, as evidenced by their friendly intercourse at the beginning. This morning at 8 A.M., when the launch went to bring water and wood, one of the two deserters, named Pedro Lorenzo, appeared on the beach and came aboard of his own volition. Since the captain was not aboard, I had the sailor give me an account of his desertion, in the presence of the two ministers and the second pilot; and he answered that he had gone off of his own accord. Asked what the other one had done, he said that he had not seen him. Questioned again whether the Indians of this rancheria had directed him or hidden him, he said no. Right then the captain arrived aboard and called said Pedro Lorenzo for a statement. When the man saw himself before his judge, he began to tremble and became confused, so intimidated that he could not say anything. The captain questioning him with his accustomed severity, whether the Indians of this rancheria had hidden him or given him assistance, the wretch answered "yes" and still other nonsense, all of it owing to the prejudice of this poor devil. Then the captain was convinced by the statement, since everything turned out according to what he had thought before the deserter appeared. The captain immediately ordered most of the crew armed, and went ashore. They arrived at the rancheria and he ordered all the houses surrounded. The first Indian he met was a poor old man, whom the captain seized, giving him so many blows that he left him maimed and prostrate. Again he questioned the deserter, asking which of these Indians had shown him the way; he answered none of them. At which the captain became angered and ordered the men to tie the deserter, and had him given two hundred lashes. All the officers of both ships resented this action, not only because of the punishment of the innocent Indian, but also because the deserter's punishment had been ordered in spite of the captain's having pardoned him the morning he appeared.

Sixteenth Day to Saturday the Seventeenth of June, 1775. In the morning the carpenters and woodcutters went ashore in order to round off some yards and a topmast that they had cut the day before. The canoe returned loaded with ballast, and with this it made three lighter loads of ballast.

Seventeenth Day to Sunday the Eighteenth of June 1775. This morning after Mass the captain went off.

Eighteenth Day to Monday the Nineteenth of June, 1775. A good share of tonight we have experienced frequent heavy showers, which kept up until 6 A.M. on the nineteenth, at which hour we began to unmoor the ship from the land side....

ACT OF POSSESSION OF THE SPANISH CROWN AT TRINIDAD BAY, JUNE 11, 1775

IN THE name of the most Holy Trinity, Father, Son and Holy Spirit, three persons and a single true God, who is the beginning, maker and creator of all things, without whom nothing good can be started or maintained. And because the good inception of anything must be in God, and for God, and in Him it is fitting to begin it for His honor and glory. In His most Holy name, be it manifest to all those to whom the present testimony, and letter of possession comes that today, Sunday, being the eleventh day of the month of June of 1775, and that the frigate named *Santiago*, alias the *New Galicia*, and the schooner *Sonora*, of the very powerful, very illustrious, and Catholic Lord, Charles III, King of Castile, of Leon, of Aragon, of the Sicilies, of Jerusalem, of Navarre, of Granada, of Toledo, of Valencia, of Galicia, of Mallorca, of Seville, of Sardinia, of Cordova, of Corsica, of Murcia, of Jean, of the Algarbias, of Algeciras, of Gibraltar, of the Canary Islands, of the East and West Indies, the islands and mainland of the ocean sea, Archduke of Austria, Duke of Burgundy, of Brabant, and Milan, Count of Augsberg, Flanders, Tyrol, and Barcelona, Lord of Viscaya, of Molina, and so on, having arrived by order of the Most Excellent Lord Knight Commander of Malta, Father Don Antonio Maria Bucareli y Ursua, Henestrosa, Laso de la Bega, Villacis, y Cordova, Knight of the Grand Cross, Knight Commander of Boveda de Toro, of the Order of St. John, Lord with Privileges of the bed chamber of His Majesty, Lieutenant General of the Royal Armies of His Majesty, Viceroy, Governor, and Captain General of the Kingdom of New Spain, President of its Royal Audiencia, Superintendent General of the Royal Treasury and the Department of Tobacco, Judge Conservator of the latter, President of his council, Subdelegate General of the income from mails of the same Kingdom.

They left the port of San Blas, one of those of the South Sea under the jurisdiction of the same viceroyalty, on the eighteenth of March

---

Archivo General y Publica de la Nacion, Historia, Vol. 324.

of this year to make discoveries, following the Monterey coast northward; commanded by Don Bruno de Hezeta, [ship of the line] Lieutenant of the Royal Armada, commander of the expedition, and being anchored in this port now again named La Santisima Trinidad, and that commander having gone ashore with the greater part of the seamen and soldiers from the frigate and schooner and accompanied Don Juan Francisco de Bodega y Quadra, [frigate] Lieutenant of the Royal Armada, by captain of the schooner, and Don Juan Perez, Brevet (frigate) Ensign, the second-in-command of the frigate, and by the Reverend Fathers Miguel de la Campa and Benito de la Sierra, members of the order of St. Francis of the Apostolic College of San Fernando of Mexico, he took ashore a cross, which, kneeling, he and all the company devoutly worshiped. The Fathers sang the canticle "Te Deum Laudamus."

In a loud voice the commander said that in the name of His Majesty, King Charles III, our Lord—whom may God, our Lord, guard for many years, with increase of greater states and kingdoms for the service of God, the well-being and prosperity of his vassals, and of the very powerful heirs apparent, and of his successors for time to come, as well as of his commander of this said frigate and schooner—and in virtue of the order and instruction that the aforementioned most excellent Viceroy of New Spain gave to him in the Royal name, he was taking, and took, was seizing, and seized possession of this land, where at present he was disembarked and which he had discovered, forever and ever, in the Royal name and that of the Royal Crown of Castile and Leon, as has been said, as a personal possession, and that truly it belonged to His Majesty by reason of the gift and bull that the very Holy Father Alexander VI, sovereign Roman Pontiff, issued of his own accord in a gift of half of the world to the most high and Catholic Lords King Ferdinand and Queen Isabel, his wife, Sovereigns of Castile and Leon of glorious memory, and to his successors and heirs given at Rome the fourth of May of the year 1593. In virtue of which these lands belong to the said Royal Crown of Castile and Leon, and therefore he was taking and took possession of these said lands, and their regions, seas, rivers, inlets, ports, bays, gulfs, archipelagoes, and of this said port of the most Holy Trinity, where at present the frigate and the schooner are anchored, and he was subrogating and did subrogate them under the power of possession and dominion of the said Royal Crown of Castile and Leon, as has been said, as a personal possession. And as a sign of possession *Velquasi;* drawing the sword that he had at his waist, with it he cut trees, branches, and grasses, and moved stones, and walked up and down the fields and the beach without any hostile resistance. He asked those present to be witnesses and instructed me, Juan Gonzalez, who am the scribe named by the commandant of this expedition, to put it in public form as testimony. Then, going ashore and taking a large cross on their shoulders, the officers carried the cross in procession, the men of the frigate and schooner in battle order with guns and other arms, the Fathers Miguel de la Campa and Benito de la Sierra singing a litany and everyone responding. After the procession, the commandant erected the cross and made a pile of stones at the foot of it as a memorial and sign of the possession of all these lands, seas, and its landmarks, discoveries, of things adjacent and nearby; and he gave this the name of the most Holy Trinity as has been said; and as soon as the cross was erected, they adored it a second time, and all prayed, asking and supplicating our Lord Jesus Christ that He might grant that it be for His Holy service, and in order that our Holy Catholic Faith be exalted, augmented, and proclaimed, and the word of the Holy Gospel sown among these barbarian nations, who until now have been turned away from the true knowledge and doctrine, in order that He guard them and free them of the deceits and dangers of the devil and of the darkness in which they are, in order that their souls be saved. Then the Fathers sang the hymn "Vexilla regis," and so forth, and immediately after that, on an altar that had been made, Father Miguel de la Campa celebrated Mass, which was the first that had been said in this land, to the honor and glory of God, our all-powerful Lord, and for the eradication of the devil and of all idolatry. Don Juan Perez, Don Cristobal Revilla, Francisco Alverez y Rua, Justo Nugue, and Bartholome Villareal confessed and received communion, and the Father Miguel de la Campa preached. When this service was concluded, for a more lasting sign of remembrance, the commandant had a tree trimmed, which he made in the form of a cross, putting on it the most Holy name of our Lord Jesus Christ, with these four letters *I.N.R.I.*, and at the foot of the cross he put *Carolus tertius Rex Hispaniarum.* And that it might be of record the commandant, Don Bruno de Hezeta Dudagoytia, Lieutenant of the Royal Armada, signed it, and as witnesses, Don Juan Francisco Bodega y Quadra, Lieutenant of the Royal Armada; Don Juan Perez, Brevet Ensign; the Reverend Fathers Miguel de la Campa and Benito de la Sierra, chaplains of this frigate; Don Francisco Antonio Mourelle, pilot of the schooner; Don Cristobal de Revilla, pilot of said frigate; Carolos Ortega, boatswain's mate; Manuel Guzman, marine gunner; Ramon de Aro, carpenter; Francisco Alvarez y Rua, Juan Maria Galafates, Justo Ortiz, Josef Romero, and Silverio del Valle, sailors; and I, the scribe named by the said commandant, attest and give true testimony that it happened as is said.

[Signatures]

Before me, the scribe, Juan Martin Gonzalez [rubric]

Mexico 4 December 1775

Extract testimony in triplicate to inform His Majesty and file this original document in the office of the secretary de Camara y Virreynato.

J. Ma. Bucareli [rubric]

TRINIDAD BAY FROM THE JOURNAL OF ARCHIBALD MENZIES, NATURALIST OF THE VANCOUVER EXPEDITION, MAY, 1793

THE forenoon of the second of May, 1793, ... we anchored within some Rocks in eight fathoms over a bottom of blackish loose sand in what the Spaniards have called the Port of Trinidad. While we were Mooring a Canoe came along side in which there were two men and on giving them some pieces of Iron & a few Nails they paddled hastily to the shore again to a small Village which we observed on the north side of the Bay. After dark another Canoe came off with a fire kindled in it, but they kept hovering at a little distance & would not venture near us till we shewd them a light, when they came alongside under the gangway & the whole Crew consisting of four men stood up & gave us a song accompanied with a dance, if bending their bodies forward & moving them to & fro with the most ludicrous gestures without changing their situation in the Canoe could be called such. They kept beating time with their paddles on the sides of the Canoe seemingly in perfect unison with their song which was a kind of a solemn air not destitute of harmony & ended in a loud shriek in which they all joind rising up their heads at the same time, one of them also broke off at intervals during the Song with a kind of shrill noise in imitation of some wild Animal. All of them had dresses of Deer Skin wrapped around their Waist & the two foremost had their heads ornamented with white feathers: After repeating their Song three times, two of them venturd on board, but no entreaties could get them below into the Cabin or between Decks & they were so timorous that they could hardly stand upright upon Deck, so they made but a short stay when they returned again into their Canoe & giving us another Song went off ashore; Their bodies & arms were marked with slight lineal scars seemingly made by cutting the Skin in various directions with some sharp instrument for ornament.

Alice Eastwood, "Archibald Menzies' Journal of the Vancouver Expedition; Extracts Covering the Visit to California," *CHQ*, Vol. II (1924), 296–297. By permission of the California Historical Society.

On the morning of the third all the Boats were hoisted out & the empty Casks sent on shore with a party to fill Water & another to cut down firewood under the direction of an Officer Mr. Swaine accompanied by six Marines as a guard.

Being detained on the preceding evening as already mentioned we on the morning of the fifth weighd Anchor & made sail out of the Bay with a light breeze from NNW ..."

EXTRACT FROM THE JOURNAL OF CAPTAIN GEORGE VANCOUVER CONCERNING HIS VISIT TO TRINIDAD BAY, MAY, 1793

THE northerly wind soon returned; with this we stood for the land, and fetched it a few miles to the southward of Rocky Point; just at the spot discovered by the Spaniards in Senor Quadra's expedition to this coast in the year 1775, which they named Porto de la Trinidad. According to the description of this place in the Annual Register for the year 1781; ... it appeared to be an eligible place for shipping.

About six in the evening we anchored in eight fathoms water, dark sandy bottom, in Porto de la Trinidad. Our station here was in a small open bay or cove; very much exposed, and bounded by detached rocks lying at a little distance from the shore. When moored, the bearings from the ship were a high, steep, rounding, rocky head land, projecting a small distance from the general line of the shore into the ocean, forming by that means the bay.

We had not been long anchored before we were visited by two of the natives in a canoe; they approached us with confidence, and seemed to be friendly disposed. In exchange for a few arrows, and other trivial articles, they received some iron; with this they returned highly pleased to the shore; and after dark, another party followed their example. These came with a large fire in their canoe;" two of them ventured on board, but could not be tempted to descend below deck, by any presents which were offered to them for that purpose.

The next morning I went on shore with a guard of marines, and a working party, in search of food and water; these were found conveniently situated a little to the southward of a small Indian village.

Most of the inhabitants of the village were absent in their canoes,

---

George Vancouver, *A Voyage of Discovery to the North Pacific Ocean, and Round the World; in the Years 1790, 1791, 1792, 1793, 1794, and 1795* (3 vols.; London, 1798), Vol. 2, pp. 240–248.

trading alongside the ship, leaving a few old women to attend us; these, after setting our people to work, I accompanied to their habitations, which consisted of five houses built of plank, rudely wrought like those of Nootka,⁴⁷ neither wind nor water tight; but not exactly in that fashion; every one of these houses being detached at a small distance from each other, and in no regular order; nor are their roofs horizontal like those at Nootka, but rise with a small degree of elevation to a ridge in the middle, and of course are better calculated for carrying off the rain. The upright boards for forming the sides and ends of the house are not joined close enough to exclude the weather, the vacancies are filled up with fern leaves and small branches of pine trees. The entrance is a round hole in one corner of the house close to the ground, where with difficulty a grown person can find admittance; I found this so unpleasant in two instances, that I declined satisfying my curiosity any further than could be done by removing the materials that filled up the interstices. Four of these houses seem to have been recently built, and were on a level with the ground. These appeared to be calculated for two families of six or seven persons each; the other, which was smaller and nearly half underground,⁴⁸ I supposed to be the residence of one family, making the village according to this estimate to contain about sixty persons. To the matrons of these rude habitations, I distributed some nails, beads, and other trivial matters, who in return, insisted on my accepting some muscles [mussels] of a very large size, which they candidly acknowledged were the only things they had to offer. After revisiting our party at work, ... I returned on board, where I found our few Indian visitors trading in a very honest and civil manner. Their merchandise consisted of bows, arrows, some very inferior sea-otter skins, with a scanty supply of sardinias, small herrings, and some flat fish. Their numbers during the afternoon seemed to multiply from all quarters, particularly from the southward, from whence they arrived both by land and in their canoes.⁴⁹ These people seemed to have assembled in consequence of signals that had been made the preceding evening, soon after the last party returned to shore. A fire had been then made, and was answered by another to the south-

Discovery and Exploration

ward on a high rock in the bay; the same signal was repeated in the morning, and again answered to the southward.[50]

Few of the natives visited the ship, though the party on shore had the company of more than a hundred. The number of the inhabitants belonging to the village seemed to be about sixty; the others, who came from the southward, were all armed with bows and arrows. These they at first kept in constant readiness for action, and would not dispose of them, nor even allow of their being examined by our people. They seated themselves together, at a distance from our nearer neighbors, which indicated them to be under a different authority; at length however they became more docile and familiar, and offered for sale some of their bows, arrows, and sea-otter skins. The bow and arrow were the only weapons these people appeared to possess.[51] Their arrows were made very neatly, pointed with bone, agate, or common flint; we saw neither copper nor iron appropriated to that purpose; and they had knives also made of the same material.

In an excursion made by Mr. Menzies to the hill composing the projecting head land that forms the northwest side of the bay, he found, agreeably with Senr. Maurelli's description, the cross which the Spaniards had erected on their taking possession of the port, and though it was in a certain state of decay, it admitted of his copying the following inscription:

CAROLUS III. DEI. G. HYSPANIARUM. REX.

We ... were confined to the vicinity of the waterside. About the outskirts of the woods the soil, though somewhat sandy appeared to be a tolerably good mould lying on a stratum of clay, frequently interrupted by protruding rocks. The grounds bordering on the seashore were interspersed with several rocky patches of different extent; these did not produce any trees, but were covered with fern, grass, and other herbage. Beyond this margin the woods formed one uninterrupted wilderness to the summit of the mountains, producing a variety of stately pine trees; amongst these was observed ... the black spruce, which with the maple, alder, yew, and a variety of shrubs and plants, common to the southern parts of New Georgia, seemed principally to compose the forest. Of the land animals we could form no opinion but from their skins, worn as garments by the inhabitants; these seemed to be like those found in the more northern part of the continent. And as to the productions of the sea, we knew no more of them than what has already been enumerated. Our stay was too short to enable us to obtain any other knowledge of the inhabitants than their external character. Their persons were in general but indifferently, though stoutly made, of a lower stature than any tribe of Indians we had before seen. They wore their hair chiefly long, kept very clean, neatly combed and tied; but the paint they use for ornament disfigures their persons and renders their skins infinitely less clean than those of the Indians who visited us the former year, to the southward of cape Orford; to whom in most respects these bear a very strong resemblance, as well in their persons as in their friendly and courteous behaviour. Their canoes also were of the same singular construction, observed only among these people, and a few of those who visited us off cape Orford, and at Restoration point. Like the other tribes on this side of America, they sang songs on approaching the ship, by no means unpleasant to the ear. Their clothing was chiefly made of the skins of land animals, with a few indifferent small skins of the sea otter. All these they readily disposed of for iron, which was in their estimation the most valuable commodity we had to offer. The men seemed very careless and indifferent in their dress; their garment was thrown loosely over them, and was little calculated either for warmth or decency; for the former, they provided whilst afloat, by burning a large fire in their canoes; of the latter they were completely regardless. The women attended more particularly to these points; some were covered from head to foot with a garment of thin tanned hides; others with a similar though less [full?] robe of the like materials; under this they wore an apron, or rather petticoat, made of the smaller animals, reaching from the waist below the knees.

Amongst these people, as with the generality of Indians I had met with, some mutilation, or disfiguring of their persons, is practised, either as being ornamental, or of religious institution, or pos-

Discovery and Exploration » 67

sibly to answer some purpose of which we remain ignorant. At Trinidad the custom was particularly singular, and must be attended with much pain in the first instance, and great inconvenience ever after. All the teeth of both sexes were, by some process, ground uniformly down, horizontally, to the gums; the women especially, carrying the fashion to an extreme, had teeth reduced even below this level;[52] and ornamented their lowerlip with three perpendicular columns of punctation, one from each corner of the mouth, and one in the middle, occupying three fifths of the lip and chin.[53] Had it not been for these frightful customs, I was informed that amongst those who visited our party on shore the last day, there were, amongst the younger females, some who might have been considered as having pretentions to beauty. The men had also some punctations about them and scars on their arms and bodies, from accident, or by design, like the people who had visited us to the southward of cape Orford; but their language was wholly unintelligible to us, without the least affinity to the more northern dialects, our curiosity could only be indulged in those few respects that inspection gratified.

EXTRACT OF THE ACCOUNT OF THE VOYAGE OF THE SPANISH BRIGANTINE ACTIVO, UNDER THE COMMAND OF LIEUTENANT DON FRANCISCO DE ELIZA, AT TRINIDAD BAY, AUGUST, 1793

August [1793], I succeeded in anchoring in the Puerto de Trinidad in lat. 41° 08′ N. Here I took water and wood. On the fourth I made sail, resolved to finish reconnoitering the piece of coast to the Puerto de San Francisco...

The Puerto de Trinidad is quite small; no vessel can be moored so as to turn with the wind or tide. The bottom for the most part is rock. The land consists of quite high and extended hills full of pines and oaks. All kinds of fish are scarce. The settlement in the port consists of four small houses of prepared timber. By a piece of sawed timber we ascertained that Captain Vancouver had been there, his men, so the Indians told us, having sawed it." All the coast explored is inhabited by heathen. We had communication with them from 44° to 41°, presenting them with baize and cloth for which they came alongside every day in their canoes. They are quite agreeable, corpulent, robust, and well made. Their clothing consists of some deerskins, although most of them go naked—even on the beaches we saw them so. They are much given to trading but are very poor, fetching nothing of value. Very seldom do they bring out sea-otter skins, but usually a kind of small reed basket, and much wild tobacco which they prize highly, because they all smoke frequently in a tube made of stone in which they cram the tobacco. No one was seen to bring fish nor to have fishing tackle, no doubt because of the ferocity of the surf on the coast. We gave

---

The original account is in Archivo General de Indias, Historia, Vol. 71. The part printed here is taken from the translation by H. R. Wagner, "The Last Spanish Exploration of the Northwest Coast and the Attempt to Colonize Bodega Bay," *CHQ*, Vol. X (1931), 313–345. By permission of the California Historical Society.

them hooks, explaining by signs how to use them, but they threw them away, giving us to understand that they were of no use. The same thing happened in Trinidad where they told us that what was good were shell fish and the large deer which they told us were in the hills. The natives we saw in this port numbered two hundred of both sexes. We found them civil and obliging, as they assisted us in taking water and loading the barrels in the launch. They were rewarded and were content. From Trinidad to Punta Delgada we saw not one canoe but many smokes which seemed to indicate that the country was inhabited. The canoes we saw resemble launches except that they are of one piece and have no prow. They are not very fast because they are somewhat overburdened with the timber of which they are made. On approaching land they let them run with a breaker and this carries them to the beach. No Indian was seen with a gun, as happens with those above, nor with anything given by any [European] power. This makes me believe that they have had intercourse with very few ships, although they were not surprised to see ours.

III

EXPLOITATION: THE FUR TRADE
1800-1849

EXPLOITATION: THE FUR TRADE
1800-1849

THE Northwest Coast sea-otter trade, a highly competitive business, led to contacts between European and American ships crews and the Indians of Trinidad Bay after 1800. Most of the coast ports had long since been discovered, and were familiar, and the various accounts of trading voyages consist on the whole of fairly prosaic journals containing comments on the weather or amount of business transacted. Vancouver wrote with an audience in mind which would be interested in the appearance and doings of the wild Red Indians of North America, whereas the post-1800 fur traders were businessmen and not scientific observers, and the romance of the hitherto little-known Northwest Coast natives had become a little tarnished.

Eleven years after Vancouver's *Discovery* anchored in Trinidad Bay, November, 1793, a trading ship, the *Lelia Byrd* which had sailed from Canton in February, 1804, arrived at Trinidad on May 11, 1804. Relations between the white men and the Indians were generally unfriendly, and open fighting broke out between them. William Shaler's account of this visit is reproduced below. Two years later Captain Jonathan Winship Jr. in the *O'Cain,* sailing under Russian contract, was in Trinidad Bay trading for sea-otter furs, paying fifty cents in value of trade goods for prime furs. Some trouble with the Indians of the bay was experienced, probably the result of molesting the women or engaging in too sharp trading, and one of the Trinidad Indians was killed. In 1808 the ship *Kodiak* entered Trinidad Bay but the crew saw neither otters nor natives, and there is recorded a second visit, by the ship *Mercury*, Captain George Washington Eayers, in the same year. No details of these last two are known. In 1810 the ship *Albatross,* Captain Nathan Winship, traded for otter furs here, but no accounts of the visit are on record. The year 1817 saw the brig *Columbia* at Trinidad, and this visit is detailed in the journal of Peter Corney, first officer of the ship. It is apparent from Corney's statements that mutual suspicion and outright altercations by both white men and Indians characterized these trading visits. The massacre and seizure of the ships *Boston* at Nootka in 1803, *Atahualpa* at Millbank Sound in 1805, and *Tonquin* at Woody Point in 1811 must have been continually in the minds of the traders, and the memory of killings and other outrages by white men must have developed the Indian attitude.

After 1817 records of Caucasian visitors to Trinidad are scanty and unsatisfactory. As mentioned in the Introduction of this study, Eugene Duflot du Mofras probably was in the bay in 1841, and there is a report of a Hudson's Bay Company ship here in 1830 or 1831. What is clear, at any rate, is that the Trinidad natives were left pretty much alone between 1817 and 1849.

The total effect of the fur traders' visits was a minor one. The Indians obtained from the fur traders metal tools such as knives, axes, needles and scissors, glass bottles, glass beads, and the like, but these never could have amounted to a large quantity though they may have been useful. Intermittent contacts of this sort do not cause any fundamental changes in culture pattern. We may suppose, therefore, that after 1817 native life ran along in the old familiar grooves, and that the visits of the white-skinned, shipborne traders became merely notable incidents in the natives' memory. These thirty years of grace were, as we shall see, only the lull before the storm which was to break in 1850.

EXPERIENCES OF WILLIAM SHALER AND THE CREW OF THE LELIA BYRD IN TRINIDAD BAY, MAY 11–18, 1804

ON THE eleventh, we arrived at the harbor of Trinidad, and moored the ship in seven fathoms, sandy bottom, and commenced a trade for furs with the Indians.[1] They appeared to be very civil, and I endeavored to conciliate their good-will by every means in my power: to what effect will be seen hereafter. In the meantime, we began our preparations to wood and water, and I went ashore with the carpenters in search of spars, which we soon found in sufficient abundance, and the latter were immediately employed in felling a large spruce, and reducing it for a foremast. The thirteenth, the savages came on board in great numbers, and, presuming on our indulgence, began to take greater liberties than they had heretofore done, and, on being checked, they immediately prepared their arms. Conscious of any superiority, I did not permit any violence to be offered them, and they were prevailed on to leave the ship; but I determined not to suffer them to come aboard again in such numbers with arms. A number of them were equally troublesome to our wooding party ashore, and even attempted to seize on their axes. Everything was finally settled, however, by means of some trifling presents, and harmony again restored. The fourteenth, I sent the second officer with an armed party a watering: unfortunately the surf was high, and they got their arms wet at landing. The Indians had been reënforced by some neighboring tribes, and began to gather around, demanding pay for the water: they were at first satisfied by assurances of being paid aboard, but, as their numbers increased, they became more clamorous, and, finally, sending away their women and children, they seized the water casks, which they immediately stove [in] for the hoops. The

---

William Shaler, "Journal of a Voyage Between China and the North-Western Coast of America, Made in 1804," *The American Register or General Repository of History, Politics, and Science,* Vol. 3, pt. I (1808), 139–143.

officer, seeing their hostile disposition, and the bad state of his arms, very prudently retired, without any resistance to their violence. On the report of the second mate, I ordered a four pounder to be fired just over their heads, to intimidate them, by showing the effect of our shot. In the meantime, a canoe came off from the village to trade, as if nothing extraordinary had happened. I was completely irritated at such conduct, after the great pains I had taken to conciliate their friendship, and ordered four of them to be seized and confined to irons. In the course of a day, several canoes came off to treat for the prisoners; I always demanded, as an indispensable condition, that the casks should be returned; they gave me to understand that they had been seized by another tribe, but, by their bringing four of the hoops, and some staves, I was satisfied that they were at least concerned in the outrage, and refused all their solicitations on any other conditions: wood and water were absolutely indispensable, but the most lay so far from the beach, that I judged it dangerous to attempt getting it down, after the savages had become so numerous, and showed such hostile dispositions. In the afternoon, I sent two officers with the boat and ten men well armed, to the watering place opposite the village; the long-boat with six men was stationed in the edge of the surf, within pistol shot of the beach, and the others went ashore to fill the casks. The savages suffered them to finish their work; but, as they were shoving off the boat, which lay aground, they ran down in a long file, firing a cloud of arrows as they approached; they returned them several volleys from the long-boat, which the savages stood with great resolution, and did not retreat until several of them fell; when they were within ten yards of our men on the beach, who were unarmed. They received a number of arrows in their clothes, but none were hurt. I now saw there was not way to get wood and water, without fighting for it, and made preparations to land again the next morning. Early on the fifteenth, I went, with two boats well armed, to the watering-place; the savages showed themselves in every direction, howling hideously, I suppose for the death of some of their companions, but did not seem discouraged. I disconcerted all their plans, however, by taking possession of a rock within ten yards of the

Exploitation: The Fur Trade

shore: its top was flat and spacious, and commanded the whole shore, the village, and every lurking place, within a sufficient distance to insure the safety of the working party in the most complete manner. [See plates 4 and 5 for a view of the rock.] Here I placed a detachment of three men and an officer, with orders to fire on every savage that should show himself. This disposition of our force had the desired effect; after a few shots they all retired, and suffered us to pursue our work in peace. Had we suffered them to assemble within reach of our guns, there is every reason to suppose they would have ventured another attack, in which numbers of the poor wretches must have fallen victims to their blind temerity.

In this manner our work advanced apace: and being convinced that the keeping our prisoners any longer could now answer no good purpose, I set them at liberty, telling them, by signs, that they and their tribe must all remove back until we were gone. I believe the poor wretches had begun to despair of ever seeing their friends again, though we treated them with all possible indulgence while in our power. As soon as they landed, the savages entirely disappeared.[2] I am certain that our conduct with these people will be attended with salutary effects to any other ship that should ever visit this port;[3] as, notwithstanding our having acted entirely on the defensive, we have convinced them of our superiority, and shown that we had no wish to injure them wantonly, but that we were able, if we chose, to take the most complete vengeance for any insult. On the sixteenth, I sent ten men well armed, with two officers, into the woods for some small spars. Unfortunately the second mate let a tree fall on him, and broke his thigh. He was brought on board senseless; I immediately bled him, which brought him to, when I set the bone and applied the bandages *secundum artem*. The savages again made their appearance on the hills, so that I thought it most prudent not to expose the men any more after our misfortune, by sending them into the woods, which afford so many lurking places. The Indians appeared desirous to make peace, and several of them came aboard to trade as usual; but we did not on that account relax from any of our precautions. In the afternoon I sent the boats to finish watering, when our fortress on the rock was still found to be necessary, as, notwithstanding their friendly demonstrations in the morning, the savages fired several arrows at our working party; but the fire at the rock kept them at too great a distance to do us any mischief. On the eighteenth, with clear pleasant weather, we unmoored and left Trinity. At noon, in latitude 40° 49′ north, saw Cape Mendocino ahead, and the port we left astern.

Trinidad is a small bay of about three miles circuit, situated in latitude 41° 3′ N., on the northwest coast of America. It was discovered by the Spaniards, in 1775, and was visited and surveyed by Captain Vancouver, in 1793. The soundings are very regular, as you enter the bay, from twenty-five to four fathoms, which last depth is found within a cable's length of the shore. The bottom is a clean black sand, with a small mixture of shells; it is entirely free from rocks, except a border of less than a cable's length from the beach, that runs quite around the bay. This bay is formed by a high rocky point, running from the northward in a direction of about south by west; within, it forms an elbow, and makes a snug cove, about three quarters of a mile deep. In the same direction, off the point, lies a high white rock, within which and the point is the best entrance; and in about a north-west direction from the point lie three rocky islets, and a range of sunken rocks, extending several miles from the land, which, with the white rock, break the swell, and render it quite smooth in the cove, where several ships may lie moored head and stern in a clear bottom, in the most perfect security. This bay is bordered by a rocky shore, with sandy beaches at intervals; behind this, the land rises very quick for about one hundred yards, which space is thickly covered with brakes, nettles, strawberry vines, clover and other herbage, and shrubbery. The top of this elevation is a plain, gently rising, and covered with a thick forest of cedars, fir, hemlock, and spruce. A little way in, the trees grow to an enormous height and size, particularly the cedars [redwoods], many of which shoot up like beautiful columns, above eighty feet, without a limb or twig. Behind these, the mountains rise to a great height, and are covered with evergreen forests, that are probably coëval with the soil that nourishes them. This high

Exploitation: The Fur Trade

land is split at intervals of about a quarter of a mile, by deep gullies, down which flow streams of excellent water into the bay. These gullies are impenetrable by reason of the thick growth of underwood and timber; the former is principally alder, which may be cut at the entrance of the gullies, and is the only wood that can be easily procured at Trinity. A little within, the forest is pierced in every direction by paths made by the moose deer [elk], which seem to abound here.

On the side of the hill, about the middle of the bay, stands the Indian village; it consists of about a dozen huts, built of a very rude kind of planks, made by splitting the ancient trunks of the fallen cedars with wedges. They are wretched hovels, partly underground, and each affords a doubtful shelter to several families. The savages inhabiting this village can ... hardly exceed one hundred persons; they are of mild stature, and a strong robust appearance. They are all clad more or less with skins of different animals; the women with greatest modesty, but the men totally disregard it, generally wrapping what skins they wear around the upper part of their bodies. They are very fond of ornamenting themselves, and with that view greatly disfigure their persons by tattooing and painting. One of their women offered me a piece of red ocher in exchange for a string of beads. I observed several of both sexes who had their teeth filed down even with their gums. The men wear their hair clubbed behind, which they increase in size by false hair;' the married women divide theirs into two equal parts; the young girls have their hair singly combed and cut short around the forehead; they have of course a much more interesting appearance than the matrons. The men were very jealous of their women; and, whether it was from fear or chastity, the latter rejected all the offers made them by our sailors, though some must have been of immense value in their estimation. Fish are not abundant on this part of the north-west coast, except during the periodical visits of the sardinia or anchovy; and although their forests swarm with deer and other animals, their rude arms render the chase of very doubtful success, so that they are forced to live principally on shellfish; their bay furnishes them a never failing supply of muscles [mussels], and the monstrous heaps of shells near their dwellings testify that they constitute the principal article of their diet.[5] Their manufactures are, very tolerable leather, made of moose [elk] and deer skins, and a variety of baskets, made of the inner bark of the cedar and spruce trees; these are water tight, and serve them for caps as well as domestic purposes. Their arms are also of their own manufacture; they consist of bows and arrows, pointed with bones and flints, spears and daggers of wood and iron; the latter are rude, being formed from pieces of iron obtained directly from foreigners, or by trade with more fortunate tribes. In their fabrication, a large stone serves for an anvil, and a smaller one for a hammer.[6] Their bows are about three feet in length, made of light wood, and very ingeniously strengthened with whale sinew, glued to the back: in the use of this arm they are very dextrous. Their canoes are of very simple construction: they are square at each end in the form of our river fishing boats, and are capable of carrying about fourteen persons. As these savages are hardly emerged from a state of nature, their language is of course barely sufficient to express the most common ideas; I was only able to learn three words of it, which seemed to be of very general signification, and, with the assistance of signs, were sufficient to make myself understood by them.

I could not discover that those savages had the least idea of culture yet they had plenty of tobacco, which they smoke out of a wooden tube. It is possible that they may obtain it in trade from some more civilized tribe of the interior.

These people, at first, utterly disregarded our firearms. They did not excite in them the least curiosity, although I took the precaution, when we first arrived, to show them the effects, by firing a cannon with shot against the rocks, and by killing several birds in their sight with our small arms. In our first skirmishes, they attempted to shield themselves against our shot with pieces of boards and moose [elk] skins,[7] and it was not until several of them had paid severely for their presumption, that they began at all to respect our fire. At first I attributed this temerity to natural bravery; but I afterwards found it was rather stupid ignorance, as, when experience taught them that they were in danger from our shot, they kept at a wary distance.

Exploitation: The Fur Trade

These poor savages greatly admired Harriet, and when we were at peace she had a constant train of admirers round her. The young bucks were at great pains to paint and decorate themselves to please her; one of them carried his gallantries so far as to present her with an otter skin: a striking instance of the influence of the fair sex on man, in his rudest state.

VISIT OF CAPTAIN JONATHAN WINSHIP, JR., MASTER OF THE O'CAIN, TO TRINIDAD BAY, JUNE 11, 1806

PROCEEDING along the coast they anchored the following day (June 11) in Trinidad Bay. The natives here were numerous and sold them some furs. The Russians were landed and the canoes sent out to hunt. They also found here great quantities of fish. Two canoes were daily employed in fishing and kept the ship well supplied. The Indians daily increased, so that it was necessary to land the field pieces to protect the camp.

The natives at one time increased to nearly two hundred about the encampment, and a strict watch was kept. The field pieces loaded with grape were ready for an emergency, and the trade was carried on by the Russians, who purchased a considerable number of otter—for those of the first quality not over fifty cents in value was paid for anyone, and several were bought for two cents of beads each.

The following day, the chief officer of the ship and the Russian commander of the hunters, with fifty canoes, were dispatched to hunt and for a further exploration. Another party was sent to fish and was very successful, while those remaining at the ship effected a considerable trade with the natives, who came alongside with sea-otter and other furs. They also brought for sale strawberries and raspberries. On the eighteenth the large party returned with poor results, having only seventeen otter. The Indians followed, and exhibited so much hostility toward them, that no attempt was made to land, and Mr. Winship, being desirous to avoid a collision, prudently returned with the party to the ship.

During the remainder of their stay in the bay, tents for the purpose of trade were erected on shore, opposite the ship, under cover of her guns. The hunters also had their camp near the tents. The next day the natives made an attack on the shore party, but were

---

William Dane Phelps, "Solid Men of Boston in the Northwest," unpublished MS, Bancroft Library, University of California, pp. 16–18.

Exploitation: The Fur Trade

repulsed by the Kodiaks, and one of the savages was killed. The ship remained here until the twenty-second, when, having filled their water casks, and laid in a good supply of fish, all of which was performed under the protection of a strong guard, it was considered better to abandon the hunting ground there, than to remain and fight the natives, and probably occasion the loss of many lives. In such a conclusion Captain Winship manifested a regard for humanity and justice, not often exhibited by the N. W. traders.

VISIT OF THE BRIG COLUMBIA, CAPTAIN JOHN JENNINGS, TO TRINIDAD BAY, JULY 24, 1817, FROM THE JOURNAL OF THE FIRST OFFICER, PETER CORNEY

WE WERE DRIVEN fast to the southward by the current; on the twenty-fourth a breeze sprang up and we made sail for Port Trinidad, in latitude 41° 3′ longitude 123° 54′ west; hauled into a small sandy bay, where we moored, sheltered from all winds, a few ship's lengths from the shore, in nine fathoms sandy bottom. This bay is full of high rocks, which are always covered with birds, and round it are scattered many Indian villages. We had scarcely time to moor before we were surrounded with canoes; we triced our boarding nets up, and shut all our ports but one, at which the natives entered, keeping all the canoes on the starboard side; and, as the Indians came on board, we took their bows and daggers from them, at which they seemed much displeased. One man (a chief) would not give up his dagger, and we pushed him back into his canoe; upon which he immediately strung his bow, and pointed an arrow at me, as being the most active in sending him out of the ship. In an instant he had several muskets pointed at him, upon seeing which, he lost no time in laying his bow down. Shortly after he came on board, and seemed sorry for what he had done, and made me a present of a fine bow. Everything being thus settled, we gave them some bread and molasses, of which they ate heartily. We then commenced trading, and got a few land furs, which they brought off, for pieces of iron-hoop, cut into six-inch lengths. They also brought us plenty of red deer and berries. In the afternoon, some women made their appearance: the people offered them blankets and axes, but nothing could tempt them to come on board. This is the only place on the coast where we could not induce the females to visit the ship. It appears that these natives have not had much communication with Europeans, as they do not

---

Peter Corney, *Voyages in the North Pacific* (Honolulu, Thos. G. Thrum, 1896), pp. 78–81, 75A–76A.

7. Graveyard and House, Tsurai Village. Drawn by J. Goldsborough Bruff, 1851. (Courtesy, Columbia University Press.)

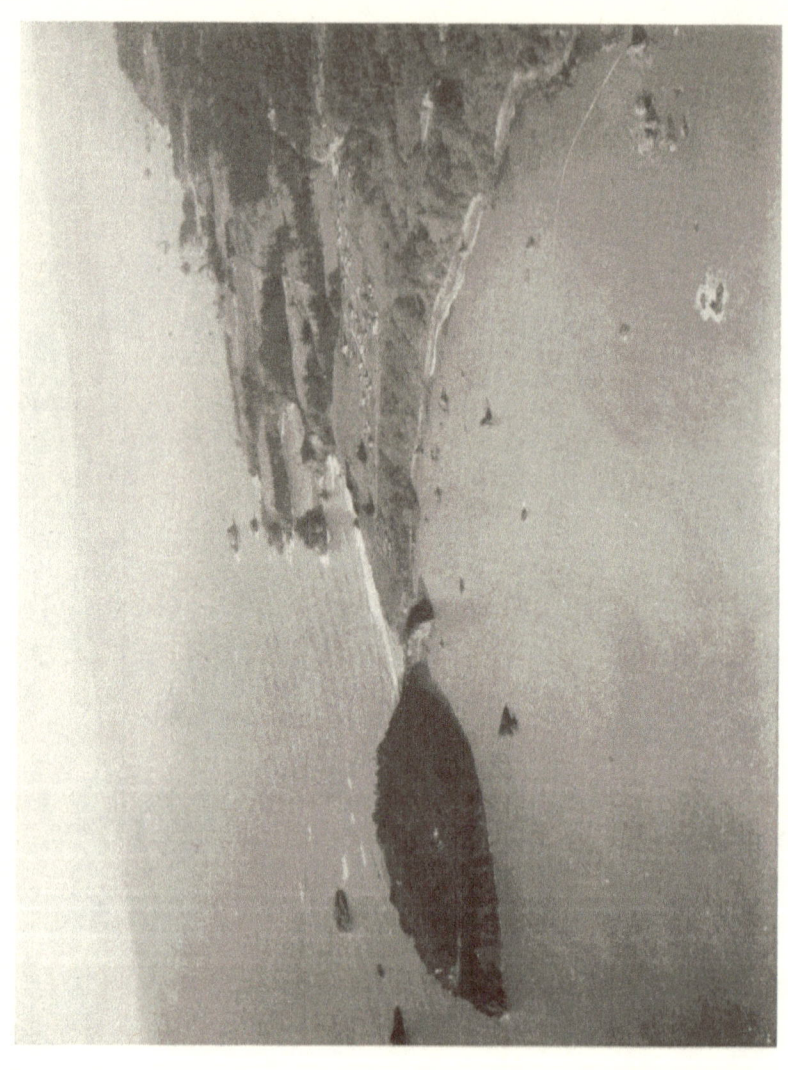

1. Aerial View of Trinidad Bay from the South. (Courtesy, Pierce Flying Service, Eureka, California.)

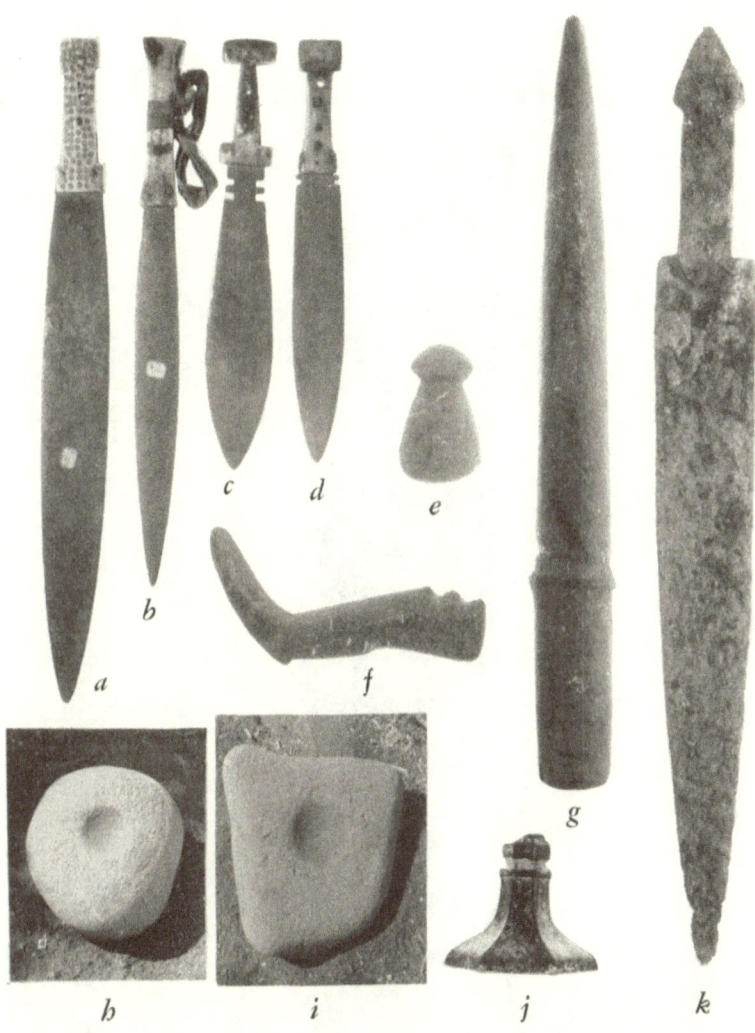

2. Prehistoric and Historic Indian Implements. *a–d*, old iron swords with elkhorn handles, University of California Museum of Anthropology; *e*, stone maul for driving antler wedges; *f*, stone adze handle, Tsurai village; *g*, stone pestle, Tsurai village; *h–i*, stone acorn-grinding mortars, Tsurai village; *j*, Sandwich glass lamp or vase base, Tsurai village; *k*, iron sword, Tsurai village.

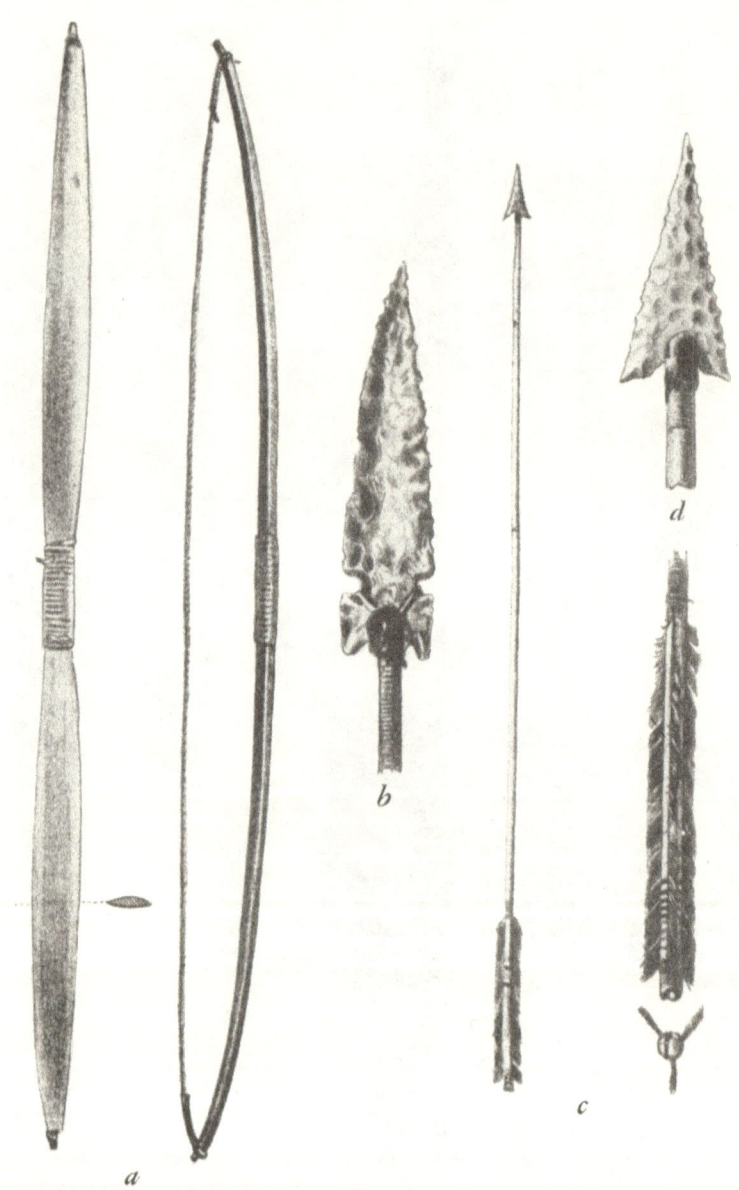

3. Bow and Arrows of the Trinidad Bay Indians. Collected before 1857 by Baron Loeffelholz. *a*, sinew-backed bow wound with grip thong; *b*, arrowpoint chipped from bottle glass; *c*, flint-tipped arrow with detail of arrowhead and feathering.

4. Aerial View of Tsurai Village and Site Area. (Courtesy, Pierce Flying Service, Eureka, California.)

5. View of Trinidad Bay from the East Shore. A Yurok Indian netting surf fish in the foreground.

6. Pages from the Act of Possession of the Spanish Crown, Trinidad Bay, June 11, 1775.

8. Grave and Sweathouse, Tsurai Village. Drawn by J. Goldsborough Bruff, 1851. (Courtesy, Columbia University Press.)

9. Plank Houses, Tsurai Village. Drawn by J. Goldsborough Bruff, 1851. (Courtesy, Columbia University Press.)

10. Willie Childs, a Last Survivor of Tsurai. Photograph Taken before 1900. (Courtesy, A. W. Erickson, Arcata, California.)

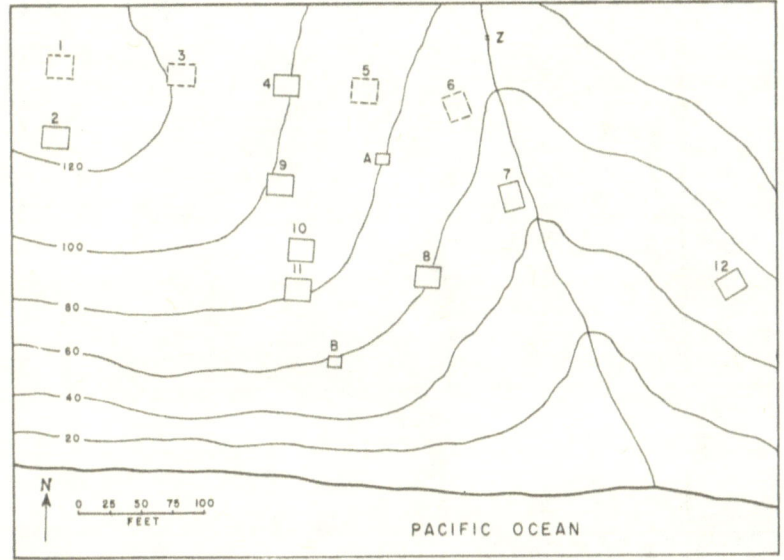

1. Waterman's Plan of Tsurai Village about 1906

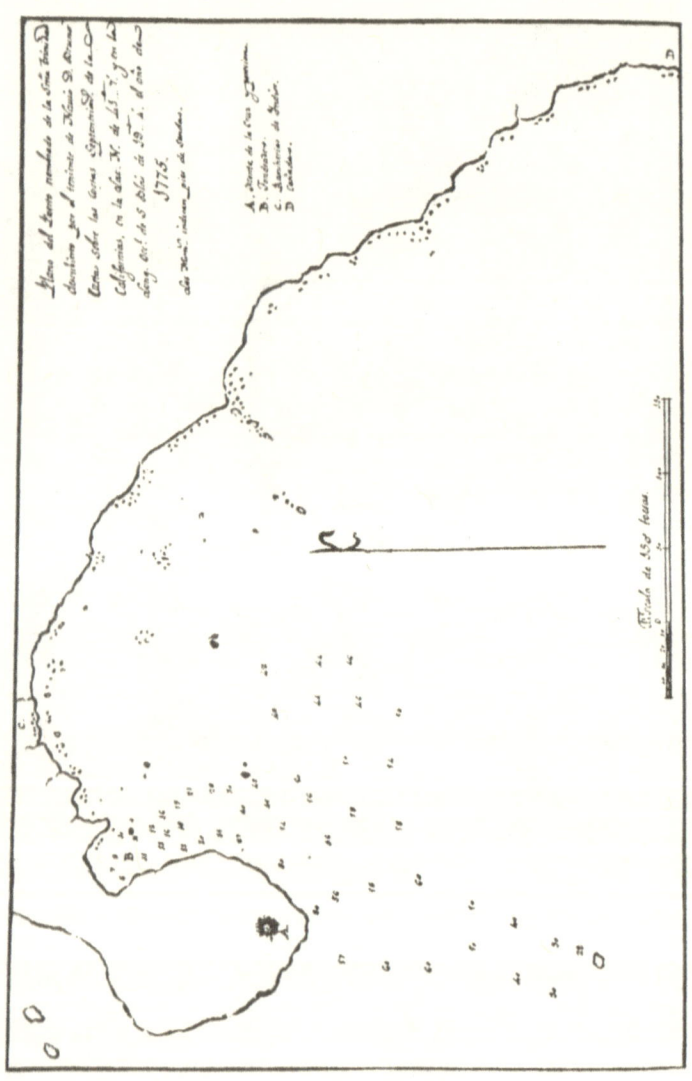

2. The Hezeta Map of Trinidad Bay, 1775

3. Vancouver's Chart of Trinidad Bay, 1793

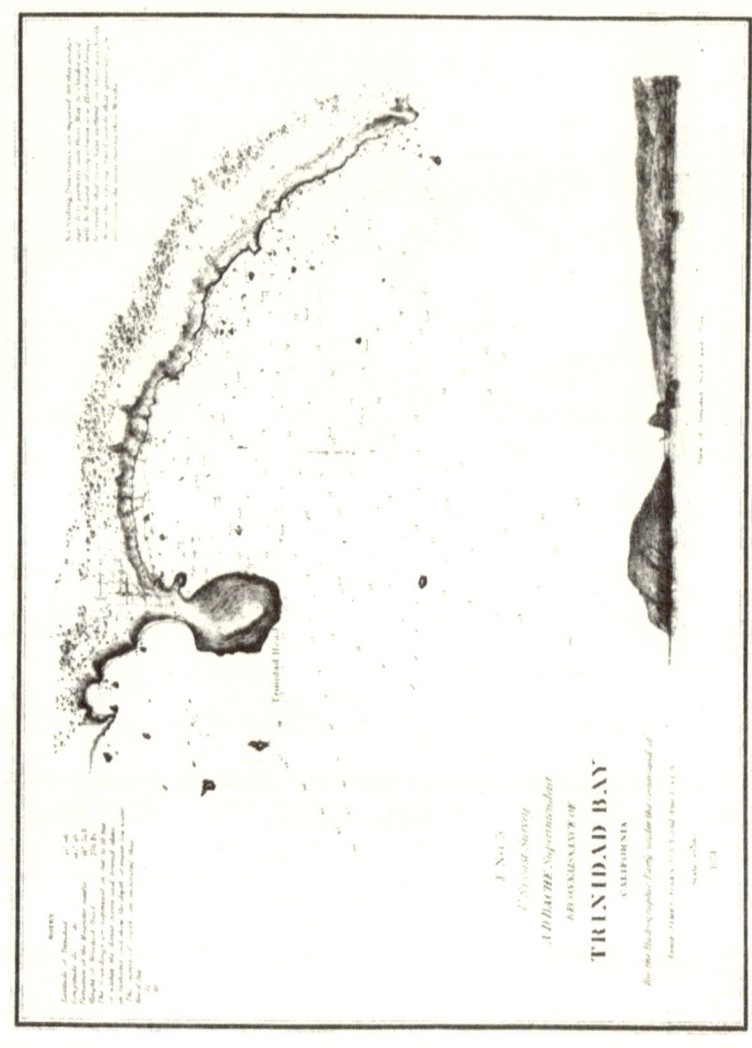

4. United States Coast Survey Map of Trinidad Bay, 1851

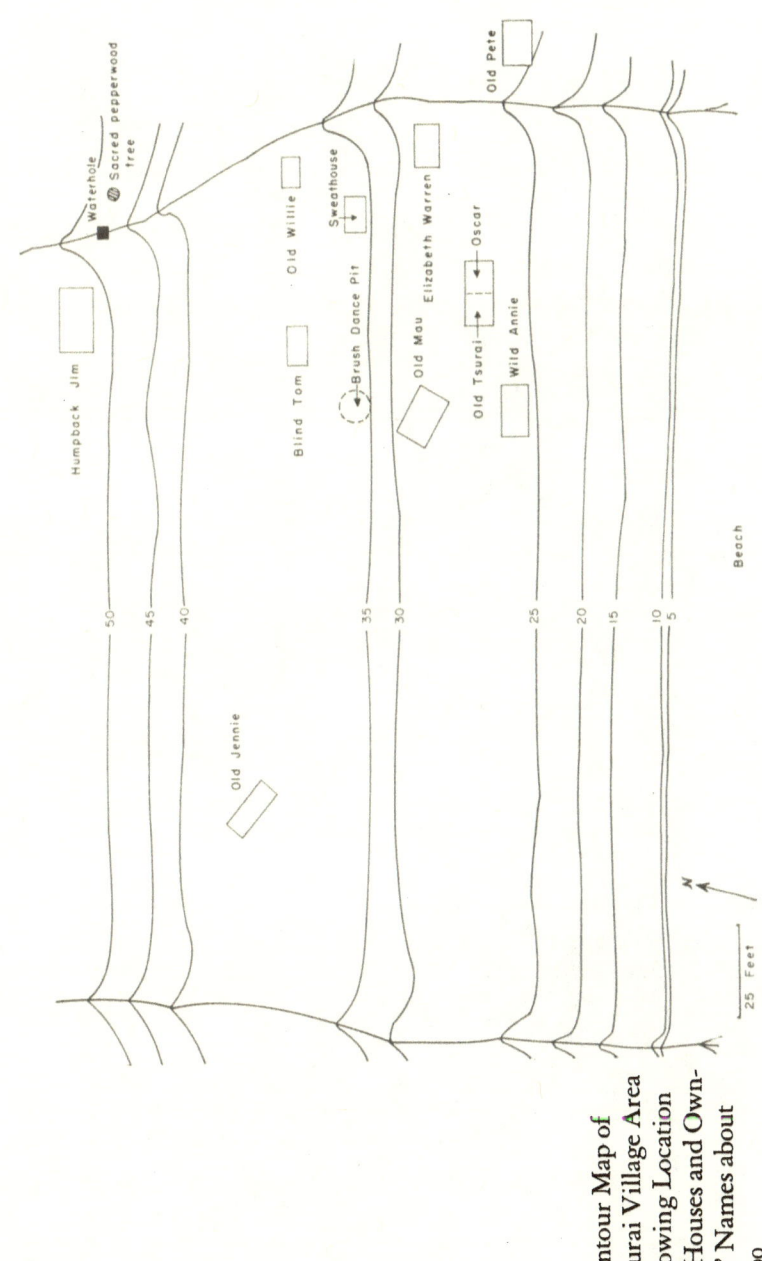

5. Contour Map of Tsurai Village Area Showing Location of Houses and Owners' Names about 1900

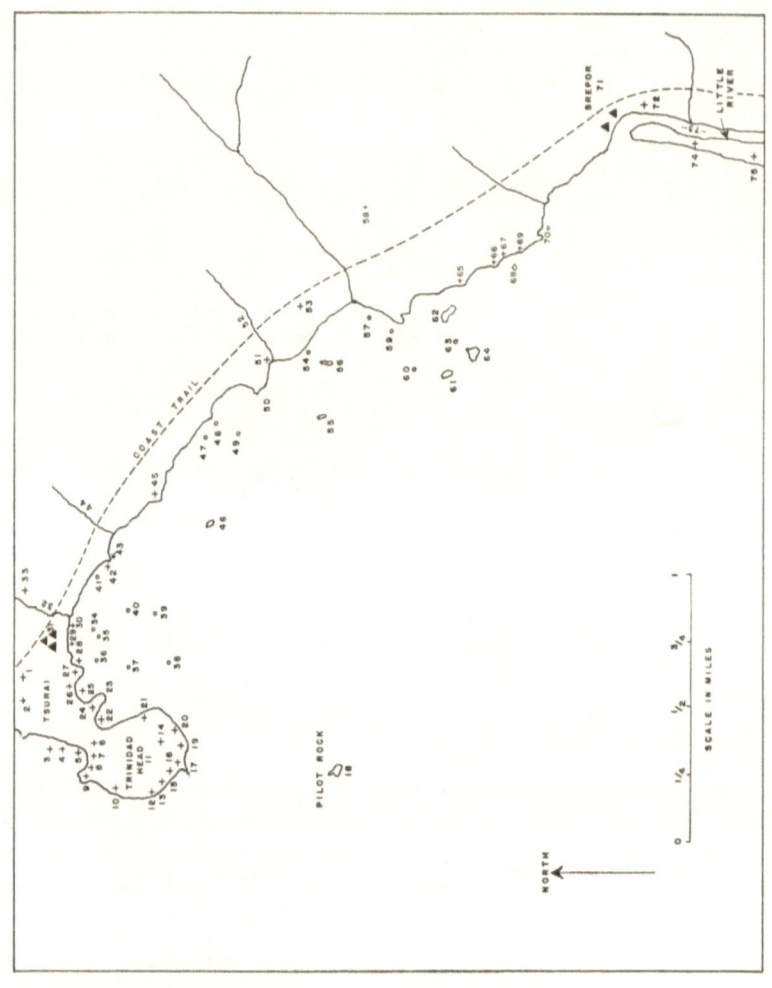

6. Map of Trinidad Bay Showing Locations of Places with Indian Names (After Waterman.)

Exploitation: The Fur Trade

know the use of fire-arms; nor have they any iron among them. Their daggers are made of a sort of flintstone, and they are clothed in dressed leather apparel, prettily ornamented with shell. The women wear a very finely dressed leather petticoat, which reaches half way down the leg, and a square garment of the same thrown loosely over the shoulders. Their tongues and chins are tattooed; the former is quite black, the latter in stripes.[8] Whether this is considered a mark of beauty or not I cannot tell, but the women here are in general very handsome and well made. We saw a cross on shore, fixed there by the Spaniards many years ago, when there was a Spanish launch driven on shore, and the Indians massacred the whole crew.[9] The different tribes in this bay are always at war with each other; they never met on board, and if the tribe which was on board trading, saw another tribe approaching, they immediately went on shore to protect their wives and property.[10] They all seem to be brave, warlike people. Their canoes are by far the safest I ever saw on the coast, being from sixteen to twenty feet long, and from six to eight feet broad, square at both ends and flat bottomed. They have ridges inside about a foot apart, which look exactly like the timbers of a boat, and serve to strengthen them very much.[11] The only words of this tongue we could pick up were, "I ai guai," which is a term of friendship, and "chilese," which means barter.[12] When they speak they put the tongue to the roof of the mouth, and utter sounds as if their mouths were full. After having bought all the furs here, on the twenty-fourth of July we weighed anchor, and, after encountering considerable difficulties, owing to the bad weather, succeeding in getting out. This was fortunate, as, had we gone on shore (there not being the least shelter in this part of the bay), the Indians were ready to receive and massacre us for they are without exception the most savage tribes on all the coast.

[After sailing down the coast, stopping at Fort Ross, Bodega Bay, the Farallone Islands and Drakes Bay, Corney went north again. The narrative resumes:]

On the 20th of August, we again stood into the bay of Trinidad, to endeavor to recover our anchor, and next morning I went with the whaleboat and long-boat with purchases to raise it, leaving the captain with only six men on board to take care of the ship. We started before daylight, that the natives should not take notice of us; it came on so thick a fog, that we only did not succeed in finding the buoy, but had much difficulty in regaining the vessel. About six o'clock in the evening however we got on board, and learnt that the Indians had been very troublesome during our absence. In consequence of their seeing but few men, they had made several attempts to board the ship, but were as often beat out of the [boarding] nets. It was of no use to point muskets at them, for they were ignorant of their effect, until some of the men shot several gulls that were flying about the ship. Upon this, they began to be less daring, and, as we fired a few muskets on approaching, they made for the shore, as quick as possible. We now gave up all hopes of recovering our anchor [lost on July 25] and at daylight weighed, and made sail, thinking it dangerous to remain any longer among this savage tribe.

IV

DECLINE AND FALL
THE AMERICAN INVASION
1850-1916

DECLINE AND FALL
THE AMERICAN INVASION
1850-1916

AT THE time of Marshall's discovery of gold at Coloma in 1848, Trinidad Bay was known only by report. An advertisement in the *California Star,* March 25, 1848, announced a meeting to be held in San Francisco "for the purpose of adopting means to raise and fit out a party to explore the region of Trinidad Bay ..." Nothing seems to have come of this proposal because everyone who might have been interested became involved in gold-mining activities. In July, 1848, Major P. B. Reading, who had gone from Sutter's Fort on a trapping expedition to the Trinity River in 1845, returned there and found rich gold placers. By 1849, large numbers of miners were at work on these streams. Among these miners was Dr. Josiah Gregg who, in November, 1849, accompanied by eight men and with extreme hardship, took four weeks to push across country from the headwaters of the Trinity River to the Pacific Ocean. Gregg's party rediscovered Trinidad Bay on December 7, 1849. The reports of the rich diggings of the Trinity River placers, and circulation of the news that Gregg's party had seen Trinidad Bay, made it desirable to find the bay by sea and utilize it as a supply port for the miners on the Trinity River. The rediscovery by sea was effected by the ship *Cameo* on February 10, 1850. In the following weeks, numerous ships entered Trinidad Bay, and on April 8, 1850, a party of men from the schooner *James R. Whiting* landed, surveyed, and laid out a town site, and erected several temporary buildings. The town boomed and at one time numbered several thousand people. By 1854 the town's heyday had passed, other ports being better suited to commercial development.

Gregg's party apparently found the Trinidad natives numerous and peaceably inclined. H. D. La Motte, who was on board the

Laura Virginia in March, 1850, describes the natives in his reminiscences, and apparently found them friendly. Other early visitors, Ernest de Massey who arrived about two weeks after the building of the town, J. Goldsborough Bruff in January, 1851, and Carl Meyer in 1851, all found the local Indians worth observing, and from their journals come details on life in the Indian village of those years. Baron Hans von Loeffelholz and his son Karl have given us the most valuable and detailed account of the Trinidad natives in their observations made from 1850 to 1856.

Aside from one statement[1] that the Indians at Trinidad Bay were numerous and troublesome in July, 1850, there is no mention of Indian troubles, or indication that the people of Tsurai took any part in the Indian "wars" of 1850–1865 in the published writings of Bledsoe and Coy. The 1850 newspaper statement indicates dissension between the white residents of Trinidad City and the natives of Tsurai; it was probably over molestation of Indian women,[2] but certainly no open altercation involving numbers of Indians and whitemen is recorded.

Occasional native homicides by unprincipled white men did take place, as Loeffelholz attests, but by holding aloof from participation in the Indian wars,[3] and because the white town of Trinidad declined to insignificance within a few years, the Indian village of Tsurai seems to have been spared extinction. Diminution of the population by intermarriage, disease, and homicide was gradual and culminated in the abandonment of the village in 1916. The extinction of Tsurai as a living town was inevitable—most California Indian villages came to a more abrupt and painful end—and it may be noted here that the period of decline was relatively gradual and nonviolent.

TRINIDAD BAY IN 1849, FROM L. K. WOOD'S ACCOUNT OF THE JOSIAH GREGG EXPEDITION

THE POINT at which we struck the coast was at the mouth of Little River. From this point we pushed on northward, following the coast line about eleven miles, when a small lake or lagoon [Dry Lagoon] arrested our progress... It was determined that we should retrace our steps and proceed south, following the coast to San Francisco... Traveling south about eight miles, we made a halt at a point or headland, which we had passed on our way up from where we first struck the coast. This was called "Gregg's Point," and is now known as Trinidad.[4]

From an observation taken on this plateau, where the town of Trinidad is now situated, this point was found to be in latitude 40 deg. 6 min. N. This the old gentleman [Gregg] took the trouble to engrave upon the trunk of a tree standing nearby, for the benefit, as he said, of those who might hereafter visit the spot, if perchance such an occurrence should ever happen.[5] Here we remained two days, living on mussels and dried salmon, which we obtained from the Indians, of whom we found many.[6]

L. K. Wood, Statement. Unpublished MS, Bancroft Library, University of California, 12 pp.

H. D. LA MOTTE'S ACCOUNT OF TRINIDAD BAY, MARCH, 1850

THE Indians came out to the vessel[1] in canoes, and made signs by drawing their fingers about their throats, and motions signifying eating. Olo Thayer said they meant to signify that they would cut our throats and eat us, and that we had better get out of the place. I got down into the canoe, and found they only wanted some beads and something to eat... These coast Indians were of a very low grade, subsisting upon fish and roots. Their weapons were bows and arrows, and spears with stone or bone heads. They made their arrowheads with little bits of Elkhorn for tools; putting a pad of deerskin in their hands to protect them. With this piece of Elkhorn they would work off a flint to a fine point, and as sharp as a razor. Sometimes they would work up pieces of old bottles in the same way, into arrowheads. They also made flint knives in the same way, very sharp. They have something like a language. I was struck more with their counting than anything else. The would count up to ten, and then go on with a prefix to each word representing a number.[2]

H. D. La Motte, Statement. Unpublished MS, Bancroft Library, University of California, 12 pp.

THE TRINIDAD BAY INDIANS SHORTLY AFTER THE REDISCOVERY OF THE BAY BY SEA AND THE FOUNDING OF TRINIDAD CITY, FROM ERNEST DE MASSEY'S ACCOUNT, 1850

THE shore and regions around the bay are inhabited by Indians who live in rancherias or settlements which lie two or three leagues apart, and are made up of four or five huts, each of which houses one or more families. The native huts are made out of boards which are not sawed but split, much as planks are split for staves. Having no knowledge, till now, of such tools as the saw and hatchet, they have managed never-the-less, to get planks from two to five meters in length and from thirty to forty centimeters in width by using fire, wedge-shaped stones, and wooden mallets.[9]

Digging foundations about a meter deep first, planks are erected on them overlapping one another. These, plastered with mud, form the walls. More planks are laid on top to form the roof. These huts have no windows or chimneys; the only opening is a hole, level with the ground, which is barely large enough for a man, crawling on all fours to enter. Such is the hut, or rather hovel, that shelters indiscriminately men, women, and children, creatures who, as a type, are close to primitive man.

By profession these natives are fishermen, hunters, and sneak-thieves. As they are not agriculturists they subsist on what roots and wild berries nature furnishes. They have no domestic animals. The men go around naked; the women wear a fly-net made of a kind of flax around the hips which comes half-way to the knees—but it is far from modest.

I have already seen several specimens of these natives hanging around the tents in the village, waiting for a chance to steal or

---

Ernest de Massey, *A Frenchman in the Gold Rush* translated by M. E. Wilbur (San Francisco, California Historical Society, 1927), pp. 56–69. By permission of the California Historical Society.

barter furs or fish for some trinket, such as pearls, bits of colored glass, necklaces or, better yet, for knives, tools or utensils.

The principal occupation of these natives is tanning the skins of wild animals, making arrows, quivers, and fishing equipment, and weaving excellent baskets. The latter, made of wood or rushes, are used for a number of purposes: as containers, for packing heavy loads on the head, and even for cooking food.

The basket is woven so firm and tight that liquids cannot filter through it but as the material used in weaving is not fire-proof the containers cannot be put on the fire. So when the Indian wants to cook his food he fills the basket with cold water, and makes a fire nearby, in which he heats some stones. These are then put into the basket one at a time, and, as fast as they cool off, they are replaced by other hot stones.[10] The cooking is then rapidly done in this simple and ingenious manner.

But certain preliminary preparations must precede what I have just described; fire must be procured. Now the Indian has no charcoal, tinder, or matches. Usually, however, some stump is burning in the vicinity or the remains of a camp-fire are still smoldering. If the fire happens to be far away the Indian takes a piece of half-charred wood, makes a hole in it, and with both hands twirls a stick quickly in it in opposite directions until in a few moments the charred stick bursts into flames....

Not long ago I met one of the men without a stitch on, carrying in one hand a sailor's knife, which he had stolen or taken in on a trade and in the other hand a bow and arrow and over his shoulder a quiver of arrows. His hair, which was tied up on the top of his head, was decked out with bird's feathers, possibly signifying chieftainship. Others are often seen wearing mantles of tanned deerskins.[11] This luxurious garment, by the way, is more frequently used as a protection against cold and rain when sleeping out under the starry heavens.

The women are the beasts of burden, as the men when travelling carry only their hunting equipment. Sometimes the women in addition to the loads of provisions which they carry in a basket balanced on their heads and tied on by a thong, and the heavy loads on their backs, have one child cradled on their shoulders and carry another in their arms....

The women, so I am informed, adorn themselves with tattooing which begins at the corners of the mouth and runs down to the chin; young girls are not tattooed so heavily as the older women whose chins are so covered by blue lines that the natural color of the skin is concealed. Girls and young matrons have only a few lines traced on each side of the chin. My own deduction from this fact is that the first tattooing is put on when the young girl reaches puberty and is gradually increased year by year until she is an old woman. Such a custom, devoid as it is of all coquetry, would never become fashionable among civilized races where the women pretend they are not a day older than they look.

Another fifty years more and this civilization will be gone and this savage, this primitive man who is now here before my eyes, will have become mythical or legendary. This is why, during my trip through this country, I am trying to learn everything I can about them whenever I come in contact with any tribes or isolated individuals.

The Indian has no beard on his face and no hair on his body. I cannot say whether this is natural or the result of some method of hair-removal. His features resemble to a certain degree those of the Chinaman and the Kanaka or South Sea Islander with the fine eyes, fairly flat nose, thick lips, and prominent cheek-bones of those people. The contour of the head is round, and not oval. This is especially true among the women. The latter are usually fat. The men in general are thin rather than heavy, and very muscular. They are agile on the trail, intrepid swimmers and divers, and quick with the bow and arrow, being able to kill a bird the size of a pigeon on the wing at forty paces.

Their sense of hearing, sight, and smell is highly developed; they can hear a man's step several kilometers away [!] and can see a sparrow at five hundred paces. They can also smell game passing in the vicinity better than a dog can. Having no adequate offensive and defensive weapons nature has given them unusually keen senses."[12] This has made it possible for them to survive, year in and year out, in this wild country where they are now living. But as the status of things has recently changed, their very existence is in peril.

The Indian is neither generous nor hospitable; he invariably tries to get something for nothing. In all his dealings he will usually try to persuade the purchaser to accept something worth less than what he is after. He will also try as a rule to get away your most valuable belongings, even woolen blankets or cooking utensils. When this fails he mutters the word *chicano* meaning trade, or barter, crossing the index finger of each hand before his face—a gesture used to express the same idea.[13] Dickering then takes place each side offering the least for the most, until in the end terms are agreed on and everyone is satisfied. From the Indian fish has been procured while he, in turn, has received glass, trinkets, and a taste for horse-trading and barter so inbred in human nature.

Up to the time of puberty the children of both sexes run around entirely naked. Young children seem to have a more intelligent air than their parents, for the adults are so preoccupied with material cares that their intellectual faculties lie dormant or grow more and more useless as these cares increase.

Mothers nurse their children as long as their milk lasts.[14] I have seen children five or six years old jump over a tree trunk a meter high to take the breast while the mother appeared highly amused at this prank. The women did not seem to object to the advances we made to these little savages. Infants in arms, on the other hand, were frightened when they saw us, and when I tried to make friends with them by offering some sugar-lumps my advances were met with cries and tears. But the little children who clustered around us were not at all diffident.

The Indians, particularly in the spring and autumn, set the stubble in the pastures on fire to destroy the insects and reptiles, and to make hunting easier.[15] Miners and hunters camping under the trees also build fires which they are not always careful to extinguish upon leaving. Things like this are what cause the fires so often found in forests and which can be seen at a great distance.

During the day we saw several herds of deer [elk] ranging from one hundred to two hundred head, but they kept at a safe distance. They are huge fellows, weighing around eight hundred pounds.

REMARKS ON TRINIDAD INDIANS BY J. GOLDSBOROUGH BRUFF, JANUARY–FEBRUARY, 1851

I WALKED down one mile below the town, and visited the Indian village; it stands in a hollow, about fifty feet above the level of the beach. Trinidad heights are several hundred feet high....
    The following Glossary of some words in the Language of the Trinidad and Tlamath indians is derived from authentic sources, and is both curious and valuable:[16]
    The village and spot occupied by Trinidad, is called *Choli*,[17] and those Indians call themselves *Alioquis*.[18]

Allumeth [olomet]	House
Aich-quaw	Sea-Lion
All*oo*-es	Sick
Augets	Noon, or mid-day
Augh-Colts	Thunder
Alcori-gaw	Dip-net, or seine
Bim!	A fire arm (taken from the sound, no doubt)
Con-nec-ti-can	Bottle
Che-wars	Hands
Chay-ger	Froth or foam
Car-taft	Rain
Cho-ho	Good-by
Che-way	Give me
Che-ah	Give me, also

J. Goldsborough Bruff, *Gold Rush: The Journals, Drawings, and other Papers of J. Goldsborough Bruff,* edited by Georgia Willis Read and Ruth Gaines, (2 vols.; New York, Columbia University Press, 1949), Vol. II, pp. 944, 954. By permission of the Columbia University Press, the Editors, and the Sterling Library of Yale University.

Chen-aw	Big
Chalice	Knife
Cah-Cah [kohko]	Sturgeon
Chi-co-itzs	To trade or barter
Chesh-e [tsisi]	Dog
Chesh	Mule
Fer-gush	Eagle
Hip-e-may	Pigeon
Horea	Arrow
Hok-koon	Tobacco
Hops-cul-waugh	Large sinews
Hoc-min-dugh	Oak forest
Hit-care	Morning (it often hits care by the bye)
Hit-care-waugh	Evening
Ish-ne-gaw	To shoot
I-equ*aw*-ya? [ayekwi]	How do you do?
Kal [kel]	You
Kegew	Theft or stealing
Kuth-wow?	What's your name?
Kich-la-gaw	Battle or fight
Kich-mike	Dead, or the dead
Ka-m*a*la	Bad
Kel-lock	Goose
Kar	Crow (this also taken from the sound,—their cry)
Kah, -am	Clothes [Ka, deerskin blanket]
Kish-ne-waugh	To-day
Kit-taw-her	Night
Keg-rugh	To the left
Kag-taps	To laugh

Lep-ro	Talk
La-gent	Buzzard
Lep-ten-no	Clouds
Li!	Look here! or calling your attention
Leptise	Hair
Lav-a-let	Snake
Mech [mets]	Fire
Mech-pa-ha	Fire water or intoxicating liquor
Mech-yoch	Sail boat (as *Mech,* in the preceding means fire, I suppose a steam craft was the first craft that visited them)
Mar-wich	Elk
Ma-quit	The male organ
Me-gues-que	Doctor
Mur-rah	Smoke
Mow-wei-ma [megwimor]	Chief, head of a tribe
Marra-po	A file
Malt-co	Head
Ma-le	Eye
Ma-par	Nose
Mapes	Tongue
Mar-pith	Teeth
Ma-par-cho	Whiskers
Mae-quire	Breast
Ma-jard	Abdomen
Milch-paugh	Legs
Match-car	Feet
Morgets	Stars
Ma-gaugh	Tree
Neck	Me

Nale-kish-la	Let me see!
Na-ermit	Duck
Neck-wich	Bear
Napo	Fish
O-quer-tsha	Mountains
O-taught-toase	Father
O-quack-ouse	Mother
Pa-gu [pegerk]	A man
Pa-poose	Child (This term has undoubtedly been introduced by the whites)
P*aa*-haa	Muscle [mussel?]
P*a*-h*a* [pa']	Water
Pop-Shaw	Bread
Poke [pūk]	Deer
Pack, Cog-ick	Blood
Quaw-er-term-er	Shoulders
Rep-ha	Sugar
Rep-sha-pa-ha	Molasses
Roree	Snow
Spa-ga [tspega]	Ears
Sc*a*lt	Earth, or dirt
Smur-ot*a*	Scissors
Slock	Large vein
Spolts	Vagina
Ser-waugh	'Scotts River'
Sco-ye-a [skui]	Good
Skeen-aw	Little
Squir-gus	Seal
Schmact-er	Bow
Shraats	Quiver
Tine-Shaw? [tinisá]	What's that? (or this?)

Tesh-a	Beaver
Taw-*l*aw	Trace
Tag-ōne	Skin
Vari-et	Black
Wors-ou-na [wesona]	Sky
War-ki-li	To see, behold
Winchuck [wentsauks]	Woman
Wo-ga	White [wogé, white man]
Won-as-la [wonoslei]	Sun
Yoch [yot]	Boat (How much like yacht!)
Yoch	Papoose, small boat
Koch-chu-wich [kohtsewits]	One
Nah-ah-wich	Two
Nar-oh-wich	Three
Choar-nah-o-wich	Four
Maw-re-o	Five
Cock-cher	Six
Cher-vér-ser	Seven
K*era*-ve-la-to	Eight
K*er*-mer	Nine
Vio-la-mar	Ten

[BRUFF'S DESCRIPTIONS ON SKETCHES]

Young Chief Shot in 1850:—The grave of a chief. With feathers around pallisade & son kill'd by the Inds at Forks of Trinity & Tlamath (the Eurooks) one hundred ms. distant, & mountainous wooded road; from whence his squaw packed him down on her back in two and a half days. Young chief named Largo—son of the Morweme (chief-[19]

In Feby 1850—when Largo's wife brot in his remains, the Indians informed the whites at Trinidad & invited them to attend the funeral. His squaw—, prepared the body for interment by washing & marking over it, many strips of black—put his beads, wampum &c. in his hands, envellop'd the body in skins; laid mats in the bottom of the grave, after digging it herself, and assisted by the whites, laid the body on bark, placing shell, &c&c—on breast—& cover'd it up. Women howling around, & old chief (the father) standing on sweathouse, directing."[20]

CARL MEYER'S ACCOUNT OF THE INDIANS OF TRINIDAD BAY IN 1851

Early in the spring of 1851 it was rumored that gold was to be found in great quantity in the north of Upper California between 41° and 42° north latitude, from along the coast to far into the interior of the Klamath River country. All San Francisco was excited as the rumor soon became so magnified that everyone firmly believed that $100 to $300 a day could be obtained there. Hundreds of persons greedy for gold made preparations for departure and left the city for the new region. Many of these were probably not so credulous as to believe completely these reports, but they thought (as people often believe what they wish to believe) that there must be some truth in these rumors. Then, too, it had become the fashion in California to follow the first rumors of new discoveries because many became rich in this way who previously had tried unsuccessfully to work the old mines and bring forth the god of the world from his dark caverns.

I joined one of the expeditions, for I was glad to seize an opportunity which offered a charming new bit of travel. I exchanged the activity of the coast city for the quiet of primitive nature, the city dwellers for the redskins, and soon departed from the scene of tinsel show and gold, where society was trying to be fashionable, to that of danger, want, privation, and resignation.

I made the journey by sea along the rocky coast on an American schooner. The small group of passengers experienced several storms and many an evil fate threatened us during the eventful trip of fourteen days.

In two days we were supposed to arrive at our destination, the mouth of the Klamath River. Our captain, however, decided that he would land us thirty-five miles away, at Trinidad Bay, for he believed that at this time of the year the mouth of the Klamath would be sanded up like that of the Humboldt [Bay].

Carl Meyer, *Nach dem Sacramento: Reisebilder eines Heimgekehrten* (Vaaren, 1855), pp. 196–236.

When in view of Trinidad Bay we were overtaken by a raging storm. Masts groaned, the wind blew, and every moment we were threatened with destruction on the rocks. Several ships which had entered the bay a few days before were faring no better. They bounced about like balls, protected only by the strength of their anchor chains. We were forced to attempt a landing in spite of the threatening danger. We could not return to the open sea as we were already too close to shore to tack without going aground.

Our captain's actions in this dangerous situation showed plainly that not only his ship but he too should have been called "Odd Fellow." The ship was making the oddest movements, jumping this way and that with the wind, and our captain showed that he was one of those daring Americans who develop the most energy and presence of mind in the greatest danger. His loud commands could be heard above the storm. In the twinkling of an eye the main and stay sails were again hoisted; he personally took the wheel and before we were aware of it the wind drove us between rocks and ships onto the near-by beach. We struck the sandy shore so violently that we were thrown against the ship's sides like volitionless atoms. Although I had been frightened at first, this made me annoyed and I resolutely pulled myself together and was almost ashamed that for a moment I had permitted my inner strength to be subdued by danger. When the ocean rolls and rages, making us its toy we become defiant and aware of our strength, but when the sea is calm and seems to be controlled by us, we often become melancholy and weak. The captain gave a second command, and the seamen leaped overboard with ropes, tying the unharmed schooner to tree stumps and boulders.

A crowd of passengers from the other ships stood on the shore helping us as best they could to bring our wet persons and baggage to a dry place. We reached the shore just as the crowd was running back and forth in bewilderment, shrieking with horror and wringing their hands in terror. One look at the towering waves explained their actions; two of the ships anchored in the harbor had broken their anchor chains and were being thrown together by the winds and waves. At first it looked as if they would smash each other, but they separated and the raging elements cast them both towards the rocks. Human aid was apparently impossible. We could hear the terrified shrieks of the passengers who were still on board. They rushed around the decks in wild confusion, naked or clothed only in a shirt for ease in saving themselves by swimming.

In this terrifying moment of catastrophe both captain and passengers were lost in a resignation where property and even life itself seemed to have little importance. Suddenly an Indian chief, followed by his tribe, the Allequas of Trinidad, appeared at the top of the cliff and hurried towards us, shouting and giving orders as he came. His appearance was so striking that all eyes on the beach, turning away from the boats in the harbor gazed at him.

The chief now began an animated pantomime. Pale and with bloodshot eyes he raised his bow and arrow in the air and shouting loudly made signs that his people and we should all join him. It appeared that he wanted to break the wind's power or chase an evil spirit from the air. This was actually his intention. We saw that we could not help the ships, but instinctively, still under the spell of their first impression, many of the whites joined in the shouting. In the meantime the ships stranded. As soon as this happened, fear vanished among the whites and as they became quieter and more self-controlled they looked at each other and became aware of the peculiarity of their actions. To suppress the secret shame they felt at their weakness they broke out in gales of laughter, turning the tragedy into comedy.

The Indians, however, were silenced; hurt and indignant with a disdainful *Quimalla woatli!* (bad whites), they turned and moved toward their village farther down towards the beach.

The passengers were all saved but in the short time of half an hour seven ships had sprung leaks and stranded and one was completely demolished. The passengers from our ship now separated and went on their ways to the gold region. But the gold rumors proved exaggerated; a speculative device invented by several ship captains to make themselves wealthy by transporting many people and much goods to the new mining region.

Trinidad Bay is still not well known. It does not assure a safe landing for ships with its island-like cape offering but little protection against the north wind. The coast is covered by dense forests and traversed by swift streams. The first settler was a German, Baron Löffelholz, who erected a large sawmill on one of the forest streams.[21] Soon an Irish farmer joined him. The first real settlement was formed at the bay in 1851 in the interests of the gold miners. At my arrival I counted ten tents; two weeks later the place had twenty-five houses, some of them covered with zinc, and many tents. It seemed as if a new harbor city had been called into being by the magic cry of gold. On my departure Trinidad city was a place deserted by man and God, put to shame by even the miserable Indian village. The founders of Trinidad quickly disappeared with most of the disappointed gold-hunters and left their dwellings to the uncertain fates. The site will once more play an important role, however, when California's demand for wood and her need for agriculture, which can here be carried on extensively, will repopulate it.

The Indians of Trinidad have their few houses a short distance south of the town on a slope abounding in springs at the edge of the ocean. I pitched my tent near them and thus observed much that was new and rare in a tribe of primitive people. Among them I learned to share many of their ideas, many of which philosphers have found to be glowing and inextinguishable even if they did not wholly approve of them.

The Allequas or Wood Indians strike me as being the finest looking and most intelligent of all the Indians of California. They are strong and muscular, with a build similar to our own. Their skin is slightly cinnamon colored, or rather bleached, like that of the ancient Incas. The cheeks of the young men and women frequently show a delicate red coloring. The head (*Homaschkwa*) is slightly flattened, the brow vaulted, the facial angle is approximately eighty degrees, the nose (*Ellek*) has a Roman curve, the eye (*Mellin*) is large and intelligent, with a slightly angular cavity, the lips (*Matella*) are not everted, the chin (*Schtalas*) is oval, and the hands and feet (*Metzk*) are small. All their features are less angular and broad than in the case of the southern Indians.[22] It is possible to detect in their faces the distinguishing features of each human race and to designate them as the facial traits of the original man. The Allequas have thick, rather smooth hair; that of the men (*Woa*) and of the children (*Papusch*)[23] is burnt off to a uniform length of one inch, which gives them the appearance of having Titans' heads. Sometimes the men wear rather long, upright braids, stiffened with some resinous fluid. These are considered an ornament, and upon festive occasions or in war are adorned with red and white feathers, which give them the appearance of a hoopoe's crest.

As in the case of all North American Indians they have but little beard (*Liptasch*). The chin hairs are ordinarily plucked out and only allowed to grow as a sign of mourning. The women (*Squa*)[24] and girls (*Wintscha*) wear their hair smoothly combed and unplaited. It falls over their shoulders in gentle waves and is fastened at the forehead with chains of shells and beads (*Agählalä*). The Allequas wear jewels in their ears; these they sometimes obtain from the whites, and sometimes copy these last in wood. At other times they are replaced by small stones which are supposed to have a talismanic property. Only those Indians who inhabit the distant mountains wear wooden or iron rings in their nostrils.

When five years of age the girls are tattooed with a black stripe extending from both corners of the mouth to below the chin. To this line is added every five years another parallel line, by which means it becomes easy to determine the age of every Indian woman. These daughters of the wilderness are totally unlearned in the fine art practiced by ladies of the civilized world of counting—or concealing—their age. On special occasions the men paint their faces with a varnish derived from the pine tree, and they draw all manner of mysterious figures and ornaments on their cheeks, noses and foreheads, by removing the varnish with a small stick while yet soft from individual portions of the skin. When dry the varnish is of a deep red brown color, whilst the bare portions retain the natural tint of the skin. This decoration is done in such a way that the face is not disfigured, but the elliptical lines running symmetrically from the forehead across the temples and cheeks give a fuller and quite pleasing appearance to the face. This in itself serves to demonstrate the skilled hand of the Allequas and their taste for more complete and beautiful human contours.

In the summer the men go quite naked; in winter they wear over their shoulders wraps of tanned stag or doe leather. They are always provided with bows and arrows which they carry either in the hand ready for use or in a quiver made of fox or beaver skin which is slung over the shoulder. The bow (*Smotah*) is made of the strong, elastic root of the fir tree; it is about three and one half feet long and is covered on the back surface with a bear's sinew, which serves to give it greater elasticity and strength. The Allequa draws his bow with the greatest ease. He also has larger bows which are used for long distance shooting. These are six feet long and when using them the Indian lies on the ground, pushes his right knee firmly against the bow when spanning, and reinforces with both arms.[25]

The arrows (*Nekwetsch*) are skillfully constructed, partly of reeds, partly of cedar wood. The upper part is furnished with two rows of feathers, drawn crosswise through the shaft. The tips are made in part of volcanic glass, in part of a fine kind of delicate pebble; frequently also of iron or ivory. The glass arrows [pl. 3, *b*] are the most dangerous. Their points are from one to one and a half inches long, three-cornered and jagged. They are fastened to the arrow by means of a firm mass of resin. If they penetrate a human body the glass generally splinters on the bones, the wound promptly festering with fatal results. The iron tips, which are supplied with strong barbs are only lightly fastened to the arrow, with the result that when the latter is withdrawn they remain in the body. The ivory tips usually bore through the body completely. Sometimes the arrows are poisoned with the juice of the sumac tree, in which cases they are only used to slay wild beasts.

Other weapons of the Allequas are the following: the obsidian hatchet or tomahawk, the club, the lance, and the javelin. The Indians are usually also provided with knives (*Tschalisch*) resembling cutlasses, made of iron which they pick up on the beach or obtain by means of barter or purchase from the whites. On one occasion on the banks of the Klamath I received the offer of a fine

Decline and Fall: The American Invasion » 125

boat (*Yatsch*) and several beaver skins, as well as of a bow and quiver full of arrows for my hunting knife. The Indian who made the offer and who would have been only too glad to barter or exchange (*Tschikwatsch*) with me was a chief, and I would have accepted his offer had not a hardened American who was present warned me that trouble would ensue if I were to accede to the request of the Indian warrior.

The Indians' whoops of the hunt, war, and triumph are very penetrating, and their shrill cry for help rises even above the raging of a stormy sea. When running at full speed they resemble a flying stag, and as a proof of their accuracy in shooting I may mention that I once witnessed them strike a ten-cent piece at a distance of twenty paces, six times out of ten.[26] The gun (*Bakschoss*) of the whites will never equal their own bows, in their estimation, as long as they can succeed thereby in filling the white men with amazement and admiration in their prowess. This flatters them and fills them with pride—a characteristic peculiar to all Indians, which is easily comprehended when one becomes familiar with their tremendous self-confidence, which is based on character and strength of will. The Indian assuages all his trials and tribulations by means of this invulnerable self-confidence, and therefore never feels consciously unhappy. Sometimes when I was in the presence of a group of Allequas, lost in the contemplation of the conditions peculiar to the mode of life of these naked men, which from a superficial point of view afford so much occasion for pity, I would suddenly be surprised by a derisive laugh, and the group would disperse as though shamed or insulted at being pitied by a white. "Don't weep about us, weep about yourself," seems to be the native's answer to the sympathy of the whites, and I cannot blame them for this.

In the summer the Allequa women wear aprons extending to the knees made of laced bast or strips of deerskin; for winter use they are made of fur or goose down. Ornamental bracelets, wampum, and colored feathers, rings, and buttons (*Tschämah*), for which they have a special weakness, are priceless treasures in their eyes.

What the calabaza [calabash] is for the native of Central America, the *haihox* is for them; this is a small basket woven out of finest bark. A mother of the Wood Indians considers a group of children as her most beautiful adornment. She carries the smallest child on her back in a rush basket and the older children in her arms or on her hips. A mother so adorned worthily symbolizes ever-productive Nature, under whose protection every living thing derives nourishment from the strength of the sun and the milk of the planets, and withers only in the presence of shade or drought.

The huts (*Mahlämath*) of the Allequas are constructed of planks, obtained either from ships which have stranded on the seashore, or made by themselves of split fir [redwood] trees. The floor dimensions of the huts are approximately sixteen to twenty feet square, the height of the walls is four to six feet, and the height of the gable ten to fifteen feet. In one corner is the door, if the two-feet wide oval hole through which the inhabitants crawl in and out can be so designated. This opening is smeared over with the blood of their sacrificial animals; it serves as a magic sign to keep off evil and to "ward off the destroying angel."[27] In the middle of the floor, which is dug out several feet, is the fireplace, over which in the roof in a perpendicular direction is a hole that can be closed by means of a cover, which serves the double purpose of a flue and a window. The fire (*Metsch*) is never permitted to go out. Over it is suspended pieces of resinous wood which when dry serve the purpose of matches, and from which the Allequa bites off splinters as they are needed. The fire is the surest sign of undisturbed family life and recalls the sacred or eternal flame of the Catholics and Jews. The Allequas sit and sleep around the fire, always with the seniors nearest to the fire, whilst the younger members range themselves around them according to their ages. The space in front of the hut is kept very clean and the courtyard is sometimes paved with pebbles. If the settlement constitutes a village the *Mählamath* stand in straight lines next to each other two to four feet apart, surrounded by a mound of earth. The graves are located in the middle of the settlement, carefully fenced in and kept sacred. No *Woaki* [woge', white man] can venture closer than a distance of three paces, for they are always guarded by women who, should any bold person overstep

Decline and Fall: The American Invasion

the limit, immediately cry out for help and scold the intruder with the words *Qui malla!*

At daybreak (*Ahwoak*) all the year round the Allequa betakes himself to the neighboring spring, where he washes himself all over, drying himself by the rays of the rising sun. The father of the family is the first one to leave the hut. He opens the chimney flue, stirs up the fire, and after apportioning the daily tasks to the various members of his family, goes off either to hunt or to gather wood (*Nakoh*) in the forest (*Thebbah*). At low tide the women go to the seashore to look for sea creatures of various kinds, whilst the children go off to hunt for acorns, roots, edible berries (*Nekbrah*) and wild potatoes (*Lokala*). The food is never preserved but always prepared immediately before the meals. Acorns constitute the main food article of the Allequas and they are prepared in the form of a stiff mush. This is placed in a haihox, rubbed on to the sides of the vessel and then quickly baked until hard by placing hot pebbles in the container.[26] Sometimes, instead of a haihox, a rounded cavity in the floor, lined with clean sand, is utilized for this purpose, in which case glowing embers are piled on the top and the mush is left until cooked. Oysters [mussels] too, are a favorite article of food. These the Allequas consume in such large quantities that it is a common sight to find great mounds of oyster shells in Indian settlements, and in the case of devastated Indian villages these finds have even provoked geologic investigations. Without the acorn, which also serves to nourish seventy different species of insects, the Indian would lead a pitiable existence. It is his chief source of fat supply and also chiefly contributes to keeping him healthy. Nevertheless, it is undeniable that in order to render satisfying a diet of acorns it is necessary to lead the existence of a red skin, with its alternations of cold and heat, as supplied by the rain and sun. The Allequa's only drink is water (*Pahha*). Civilization has not approached closely enough to give them other drinks in accordance with the Christian teaching of Solomon's proverb, "Give strong drink to those who should be killed, and wine to the sad souls, that they drink and forget their misery and think no more of their misfortune."

The Allequas lead a solitary, quiet and contented existence; it might be called a close-knit family life, although the family is never united for long. The man is often away hunting, the wife remains at home with her children or at the graves of her loved ones. The chief (*Mauhemi*) is very greatly respected; he has control over the actions and customs, life and death of his subjects, and his power is passed on to his first born. Polygamy is permitted the chief; frequently he is the father of a very large family.

After an Allequa has chosen his future mate from among the belles of his tribe and wishes to marry her, he must show the Mauhemi a chain of shells of an arm's length. This consists of large, long, black shells, the size of a thumb, furnished with a natural hole. These shells (*Hiaquay*) are only found in the extreme north and are obtained from other Indian tribes through trade or war. On account of their rareness these shells also represent in the eyes of the Allequas the highest form of money (*Tschikh*).[29] In addition to this chain of shells a bridegroom must be the possessor of several of the red feathers[30] such as formerly were part of the costly mantle worn by King Kamehameha, as well as of the one owned by the present monarch of the Sandwich Islands. If the chief thinks that the purchase price is sufficient the Allequa is permitted to take home his bride and the young wife receives the said jewels as her dowry, together with other ornaments. The chain of shells and the costly feathers thereafter become the hereditary property of the first-born son, so that at a later time he will be able to marry without difficulty, whereas his younger brothers will be compelled to struggle in order to obtain the costly purchase price.

The conjugal life of the Allequas is very chaste. As in the case of all other wild creatures, they mate only in the spring, and from this union regularly spring strong, healthy children who are nourished at their mother's breast.[31]

Although unfamiliar with the abstract conception of morals, the Allequa faithfully observes and practices its precepts, and although only dimly conscious of his superiority to the white man in this respect, he instinctively realizes his moral shortcomings and calls him "pale-face" or "weakling." He and his wife treat with contempt the bold, lewd "pale-face"; the young girls blush with shame and shrink back in horror when a white man jests about their nakedness or stares lustfully at them. This is a sign that modesty is inherent in the human race though art must first awaken it in a simple nature. In this the maidens resemble Diana who responded to no sensual feeling but directed her feelings and glances towards the distance and seemed heartless and cold rather than sensitive and gentle to the pleasures of love. The Indians of North California are on a higher moral level than are their tribal relatives of the east or of the softer south. But foreign customs which have been impressed upon them, concepts of society and religion, which when brought into sudden contact with a primitive form of human life are bound to be both misunderstood and misapplied, have served rather to ruin than to elevate the wild inhabitants of the forests and plains.

The Allequas harden their children at an early age and inspire them with profound respect for the divinity, old age, and the Mauhemi. Their customs are wild, but in their own untamed manner they respect that which is honorable. The father trains his son to be a hunter and a warrior; the mother teaches her daughter to be a diligent housewife, although she is also taught the use of the bow. The children are trained to be merry and alert if their life is not to become a somber dream, as it so often the case with uncivilized peoples. The boys are not permitted to indulge in sexual intercourse until they have attained complete manhood. They are taught to vent their energies in manly occupations and must make the acquaintance of the Muses of Nature before they are permitted any intimacy with the Graces.

The various tribes of the Allequas which inhabit the northern regions of Upper California do not always live on mutually amicable terms; they have frequent disputes, a condition which is readily understood when one considers that with them, as with all Nature's children, it is not law, but might which is held to be right. Therefore they fight in every way, in the open and in ambush. During my stay in Trinidad the son of the Mauhemi was killed while hunting by the Wood Indians on the Klamath River (*Rhäkwa*).[32] This caused a terrific commotion among the Allequas of Trinidad (*Tschura*) and they swore bloody revenge on their enemies

(*Ihnek*). Twenty well-armed archers hastened into the mountains along hidden paths (*Layapp*), led by the unhappy father, their sixty-year-old chief. They roamed all over the region for several days, killed some of their enemies and burnt down their dwellings. They found the corpse of their relative fearfully mutilated and scalped, and brought it back to their burial place, together with the blood-soaked earth on which the body had lain. Here the whole tribe gathered every morning for a whole week, mourning for the dead and weeping and lamenting in a monotonous dirge. The corpse was not buried until heavy decomposition had set in. The mourners brought all the possessions of the dead man to the grave, which they encircled with small baskets and shells, strewing flowers over all.

After a time these little baskets frequently become converted into dainty flower vases, for the bases when brought into contact with the moist earth rot away and plants sprout up through the opening in great profusion. A flower sprouting out of a basket is a lucky omen and indicates that the deceased has reached Paradise. This profound veneration for grave flowers is a marked characteristic of the Allequas. Often the maidens of the village go to pick the flowers growing on the graves of their dead relations. They look at them with the greatest respect and, obeying an innate impulse for grace and beauty, place them in their hair as an adornment.[33]

The religion of the Allequa teaches him to "love his relatives even after death, so that they may think of you when they reach the realm of eternal life, whence they have come and whither all men return." The origin of this religion appears to be the longing for the long lost state which preceded this earthly existence. For the Allequa, as with all primitive peoples, the hereafter is only a more glorious repetition of this world, from which all trouble will have vanished; it is the happy hunting grounds where are assembled the shades of the departed. But he also believes in the transmigration of souls who, when weakened through an evil life on earth assume after death some animal form, varying in type according as they were more or less good or bad, strong or weak. Only after a long period of such atonement can these beings enter the celestial paradise. In particular, the Allequa believes that his favorite "prairie dogs" and their mongrels are the incarnations of these souls. He hopes by constant association with these animals, or by eating them, to absorb their souls into his own. He thinks that by degrees a soul can pass from a lower animal form to a higher and that when in a state of complete perfection it may reënter a woman's fertilized womb. These transmigration beliefs of the Indians are very involved, and it is very difficult, in the absence of an exact knowledge of their language, to investigate the real significance thereof,[34] as well as the real meaning of the other esoteric religious customs of the Allequas; for they strive to conceal them even from their most trusted alien friends.

Certain animals and fruits possess religious significance in the eyes of the Allequa, and as in the case of the taboo of the inhabitants of the Sandwich Islands he is forbidden to partake of them. He is permitted to eat of the flesh of the stag (*Mauwitsch*), of the sea lions (*Swega*), the hedgehogs (*Kahwin*), salmon (*Wuimosla*), geese (*Kwakwa*), ducks (*Nayamed*) and all scaly fish. Pork and fat bear's flesh (*Negwitsch*) is forbidden and only permitted to old women. I was astounded at the repulsion and hatred aroused in these Indians by the sight of the donkey. Every time it appeared to them as a fresh misfortune when a white arrived in their midst with one of these animals. I was unable to discover whether this had a basis in religious superstition or not, but the suggestion forced itself upon me that the Allequas hereby appeared to demonstrate a bond of union with the Phoenicians and the Egyptians, for these races, as is known, symbolize in the donkey, as in the pig, the universal conflict or typhoon, which also corresponds with their conception of evil.

According to the strictest interpretation of anthropophagy the Allequas are cannibalistic and partake of human flesh or blood, namely, when they eat their own lice for they are of the opinion that by absorbing this parasite they are able to take to themselves some portion of a departed soul which has entered into some particular form of transmigration, or at least to be able to absorb that individual's character. An example of this is found in the case of certain other Indian races who for the same reason drink the ashes of their departed ones with water.

The Allequa worships the sun (*Woanuschla*) and moon as symbols of subordinate divinities, and he prays to them aloud and in a sing-song manner when he is walking, running, or dancing. This occurs on the occasion of festivals, and is accompanied by such a state of excitement that one is justified in comparing this religious practice with the modern cases of revival occurring in certain sects among civilized races, where consciousness is completely deadened and the religious ideas become confused, these cases serving to show what an indispensable factor the sensual element is in religion.

The evil spirit (*Magäschkwa*), on whom the Allequa has bestowed the color white, rules in the air and manifests his terrible anger in the storm; the good spirit he worships in the luxuriant meadows and groves, identifying him with the spirit of Nature, in whose presence he alone is happy. That is the reason he is always out of doors where he feels happy.

As with many of his tribal relatives, the Allequa holds the northwest trade wind in religious veneration. It indicates to him the direction whence, according to his own opinion and mythical hearsay, all the white races as well as his own have come.[35] Because as this appears to indicate he believes in a common descent of all human beings, he shows a disposition to live with the whites on a peaceable footing and is willing to be friends with them if their attitude toward him is kind. He takes delight in the good customs of the white man, in his skill and manner of dress, and sometimes is even glad to imitate him in the latter particular. He has already given distinctive names to the various articles of clothing (*Woa-Kaya*). So, for instance, *Akah* is hat; *Kahlin,* cover; *Släkwa,* coat; *Tschäkwa,* trousers; *Noahai,* shoes. With his very simple but flexible language, so rich in onomatopoeia, he readily finds expressions for new ideas. Inflection and gestures greatly help to supplement his conversation, in which he is very animated. His sibilants are particularly effective, and produced by pressing the tongue against the teeth of the lower jaw and pressing the air between this and the hollow cheek, which is easily done thanks to the Indians' agile tongue. Nevertheless the language of the Allequa is limited and inadequate to his need of expression, considering that he is usually endowed at birth with no inconsiderable mental powers.

I soon learnt some words of the Allequa language, and conversed with my wild friends to the extent of my powers. Certainly a good deal of patience was needed for this, but I luckily possessed considerably more than do the Americans, who are quite indifferent to the Indians and think that they are not human. For this reason the Indian hates the American,—to be correct, he despises him. Although he recognizes no national difference other than that of color, and simply divides men into good and bad (*Skuya* and *Quimalla*), nevertheless he has already discovered that the Americans are worse because more hard-hearted. No wonder! Have I not with my own eyes seen Americans steal women and girls and treat them as slaves, and compel men to serve them as guides and burden bearers?

The Allequas possess a developed form of phonetic hieroglyphics, but they draw their concepts in symbolic, or more frequently in kyriological pictures. I would often ask the chief the name of some object or other (*Tennäschä*), whereupon he would draw illustrations in my pocket notebook with a pencil with which he was always wanting to scribble. This and many other striking examples made me remark the Allequas' intelligence and acquisitiveness. The first thing they ask their white friends to tell them is their name. *Kaluschkwa?* (What is your name?). They, too, are willing to give their names, which usually have reference to some external or internal characteristic of a person and do not sound bad. Thus, for example, the following are some of the men's names: Tetawa, Neeschak, Tschimma, Schenna, Mawema, Tenna; and women's names: Negawa, Homika, Tschäkscha, Mirza, Seinna, Peyakwa.

Very acceptable as presents in the eyes of the Allequas are sugar and bread (*Papschu*), which they greatly enjoy, but usually not without paying the price of this unfamiliar food in the shape of internal pain. Then they get angry with the donors and *Cigana Papschu!* (give me bread!) is followed by, "Quimalla woaki!" (Bad white man!). I was sometimes able to cure Allequas of these and other troubles, for which reason they venerated me as a doctor, an individual, by the way, upon whom not very flatteringly they bestow the same name, doctor, (*Mahgäschkwa*) as that given to their devil or magician. Thus, Mahgäschkw' with them means medicine; whilst Mahgäschkwa is the source of disease and at the same time its healer, a power equally feared and venerated. Their knowledge of medicine is limited to an acquaintance with very few substances, considered panaceas, and subject to combination according to certain prescriptions, such as the magnetic Baquet. They serve as charms, but their idea of medicine is so inadequate and confused that it is surely not to be wondered at that the doctor and the devil convey the same idea to them. Though the Allequas lack art, nature serves them the more. Animal magnetism, although not recognized as such, seems to play an important role in the lives of these and other Indians. Think of the hypnotic influence on wild animals of a sharp look, like the snake fixing his eye on the frog which he wishes to devour; of the gentle stroking of a sensitive person, then confusing him with tobacco, touching his body and breathing on it so as to impart to him prophetic ability; and then think of the wild, stormy religious dances in which the dancers change partners, embracing each other while looking sharply into each other's eyes. It is not astonishing that the miracles springing from such experiments based on the phenomena of animal magnetism often gave rise to religious theories among the Indians, just as in recent times the same thing occurred among the Christians with their "somnambulistic table" about which Galileo could say: *e ppur si muove!*

Upon taking leave of the Tschura-Allequas there was no end to their *Ayaque!* (greeting) and *Tschohho!* (farewell). The old Mauhemi told me to come again soon, and in the meanwhile offered to sell me his daughter Negawa who, he declared, already belonged to me in part, as I had made a sketch of her. However, even if I had been able to contemplate that felicity, like a happy Endymion, by what means would I have been able to obtain the costly price of purchase, in particular the string of [dentalia] shells?

I took my departure, not without a secret feeling of anger at the reflection that, instead of trying to win these good people to a sensible form of civilization, they were being subjected to a continually increasing persecution, nay, a systematic war of extermination.

BARON KARL VON LOEFFELHOLZ' ACCOUNT OF THE TSOREI INDIANS OF TRINIDAD BAY, 1850–1856

THE history of the inhabitants of California is divided into three periods: (1) the time of the original inhabitants (Indians) before the extension of the Spanish rule; (2) the period of Spanish, that is, Mexican rule; (3) the occupation by the United States.[86]

This is not intended to be a learned discussion about the Indians of California, which would present great difficulties because of the lack of accurate and extensive information on the past of these people. I am only reporting on how, over a period of six years, [1850–1856] I learned to know, through their appearance, their daily life, and their customs, Indians who came in contact with whites only recently; whereas Indians who have been associated for a long time with whites and have intermarried with them are less interesting. It is fortunate that our California Indians are, on the whole, a people of much gentler nature that the Indians of neighboring Oregon, the eastern Sierra Nevada, and northern Mexico.[87] Aside from their natural tendency toward wildness, the contact with treacherous Mexicans and merciless American pioneers on the Far Western frontier was of no advantage to the last-named tribes. The barren regions of the interior did not permit peaceful occupations—farming or stock raising. From the whites they received weapons and became acquainted with possessions which disposed them to thievery. The many wild and tame horses made their quick movements and attacks easier. Neither Mexicans nor Americans, with their insufficient forces, could prevent these raids under the local handicaps. As a result of wrongdoing on both sides there was a tendency toward mutual reprisals on the part of both Indians and whites; and this situation can only be ended by

---

Karl von Loeffelholz, "Die Zoreisch-Indianer der Trinidad-Bai (Californien)," *Mittheilungen der Anthropologischen Gesellschaft in Wien*, Vol. 23 (1893), 101–123.

the gradual extermination of the redskins. The Oregon Indians were perhaps not so wild by nature but, roused by the injustice, oppression, and persecution by the large white population of Oregon, they proved dangerous and unrelenting enemies. They also had good horses and were well armed, being generously supplied with arms by English traders of Vancouver Island. All these tribes, however, are not further discussed in this paper.

The earlier missionary fathers, by the employment of the natives in all sorts of work, gradually and peacefully civilized the California Indians living near the missions, so far as this was possible with the not ideal example of the white Mexicans and Californians at hand. Intermarriage between whites and Indians furthered this rapprochement and easily increased the missions' influence and power over the latter. But this relation with the Indians extended to only a very small part of California; from the coastal ranges west to the sea, around San Francisco Bay, and north for about fifty miles.[38] On some of the large ranches, for instance, on Sutter's estate near Sacramento, the farming was carried on by several hundred Indians living there *en famille;* but this practice ended after the founding of the city of Sacramento. On the other hand, the owners of old Fort Ross always used the Indians living near by in this fashion and, owing to the lack of white labor, these natives demanded compensation. But these proprietors complained of the Indians' lack of zeal, of the necessity of urging them on, of their tendency to disobedience, and regarded them, considering their production, as rather expensive workers, since, although they did not receive wages, they got complete support for their whole families with blankets, presents, etc. In spite of this, because of the high wages for white labor in California, Indian labor is cheaper, especially in occupations where the work can be well measured by time or where it is done on a contract basis.

The Indians of California did not like to roam very far; everywhere they found enough game, fish, and sometimes also vegetables for their needs. Thus, three-quarters to four-fifths of the red population were not familiar with whites, except perhaps for some exploring expedition made by the Spaniards or Americans.

Decline and Fall: The American Invasion » 137

Their self-sufficiency and small total number made fighting among themselves rare; in character they were thus more peaceful and gentler than the border Indians. When the territory was conquered by the Americans and plains, mountains, and valleys were overrun by the whites (especially after the discovery of gold), the original inhabitants were found to be completely uninformed about anything which lay outside their range of view. Acquaintance and communication proceeded without disturbance because the Indians were outnumbered and owned nothing which would rouse the cupidity of the newcomers. Vice and shady dealings appear wherever people of all nations and sentiments congregate and money circulates in abundance. Wild spirit breeds roughness, freedom of action, and crime. It was especially the attacks on morals and family life which sometimes caused discord between whites and Indians and violence, leading even to bloodshed. The American's least virtue is consideration for and protection of strangers or original inhabitants of the places to which he comes, or a scrupulous treatment of minorities and a regard for weaker peoples. And the majority of them care even less about the physical and spiritual well being of their fellow men, especially of colored people or Indians. If Germans or Frenchmen, for instance, had occupied California, these men of nature perhaps would have been treated better and have received more justice. They might have been helped and instructed in the useful occupations of white culture.[39] They might have been convinced by good example and by humane treatment of the value and dignity of civilization and might have been trained from youth to be useful inhabitants of this fertile land. But for this there was neither time nor inclination. The Indians saw and learned more bad than good, and the elevation of the morals and the improvement of the physical conditions of these poor natives is that much more difficult now than it would have been at the beginning.

More serious quarrels and damage to the property and person of whites led the government to try and prevent contact between whites and Indians. Large, free tracts of land, far from where white people lived, were chosen (Indian reservations) and attempts were made by gifts and persuasion to induce scattered tribes and families to move to these places. Commissioners were appointed in many counties for this purpose, sums of money were put aside for the building of homes, the buying of cattle, farming equipment, and seeds. In the first years food was distributed and the natives were kept at farming. There are about ten of these Reservations in the United States. All this was done with good intentions. But if one knew the life of the savage, his attachment for his old home, his desire for freedom, and for the privilege of hunting and fishing freely at places where he rarely meets other people, then one could foretell the opposition of the Indians to such institutions. Many of them disappeared secretly, others could not be made to leave their homes. Depression, nostalgia, sadness troubled their minds and, among the older people, often led to early death. These governmental actions, however, should be regarded with the utmost tolerance, and if only a quarter of all the natives follow government orders and survive the period of readjustment, the well-meaning and noteworthy efforts of the government are well rewarded. I consider ill-advised the collection of such a number of people, often almost a thousand individuals. One should first bring some suitable families from each tribe to some near-by settlement, then permit some of them from time to time to visit their homes under supervision and try to attract more young people of ten to fourteen years, but in any case the older ones should be permitted to die quietly in their homeland. Once these few families and some young people—say, one hundred to one hundred and fifty persons—have lived this changed life for some years and have become accustomed to their new abodes, then the others can safely be allowed to follow. I have often noticed that the Indian is like a child in many ways and should be treated as such. Good sense, kindness, firmness, and good example, sincerity and frankness, as well as interest in his troubles and sorrows, make a great impression on him and bring out affection for his fatherly benefactor and ensure his attachment and obedience. A different way to civilize without injuring them would be to have regularly appointed persons in certain districts plant in the various Indian settlements patches of potatoes, corn, carrots, etc., foods to which the Indians have rapidly become accustomed. These people would then teach and supervise farming. Diligence and zeal would be rewarded with small gifts or distinctions and gradually large areas could be cultivated. In this way the people would become less dependent on the diminishing hunting and fishing and the products of the seashore.

The surest and most natural way to accustom the Indians to work and civilization and to change them into useful people is keep them busy from youth on, according to the proverb, "as the twig is bent, the tree is inclined." As an Indian chief told me himself, when I remarked on the rapid tiring of his people in farming, etc., and pointed out to him the advantage of farming for himself: "... they realize it and that their children should be trained in this work ... but for the older people it is too late to accustom their bodies to this kind of work."[40]

The different tribes of California Indians differ on the whole little from each other in their appearance and mode of living. The northern tribes are more lively and have more spirit. They are proud, better looking, and of a larger build; they are bolder and resemble the Indians of Oregon to whom they are apparently related. The tribes of the Siskiyou Mountains between the sea and the upper Klamath River made much trouble for the Americans in 1855 and 1856.[41] Otherwise, there has been little open and lasting hostility from other California tribes, even though single deeds of violence are not infrequent. The members of these northern tribes make good helpers for mule packers at about one-fifth the wage for a white assistant. The people of the southern tribes, who have intermarried with Mexicans, are used as herders and drivers by animal traders and are also employed in farming. The Indians of the rest of the country live for the most part in remote, widely dispersed, small Indian villages, in constant fear of brutal outbreaks of violence by drunken miners, and cling to their old customs. It was these whom the government later tried to bring together and settle on the Reservations.

I had the opportunity of associating for several years with the Indians of the coast about two hundred and fifty miles north of San Francisco and am reporting on them as follows (Appendix, 1.)

[The original Loeffelholz account has fifteen appendices. These comprise pp. 158–179 of the present account.]

The build of these Indians is not large but they are broad-shouldered, of erect posture and gait, and walk with short, rapid steps. Facial build varies a great deal, but they always have prominent cheek-bones, a broad mouth, dark eyes, and a longish nose with broad wings. In the women there is a tendency towards corpulence, probably owing to the large amount of fish and seal fat in their diet. The thick, black, wiry hair, which reaches far down the forehead, is worn by the men half long, held over the forehead by a string; the women wear their hair in double pigtails (See Appendix, 2.)

In the summer the men go about their settlements entirely naked or clothed only by a light fur about the loins. In the winter they wrap themselves in the hide of elk, mountain-lion pelts, or deerskins and always carry quiver, bow, and a long, two-edged knife on a handstring. On their heads, both sexes wear small, round grass caps, woven in nice patterns. These are not worn by the men for the hunt, in war, or on other serious occasions. Recently they have learned the use of European dress and wear shirts, trousers, hats, and often footwear.

On festive occasions the important men wear a band of white seal, to which they sew the red crest of the black woodpecker and attach various ornaments made from other animals. They also stick feathers of hawks and red woodpeckers in the headband and in the erect feather headdress made of the plume of the silver heron. They paint their faces, arms, and chest with cinnabar and also with white or blue paint.

The women always wear around their loins a soft leather skirt which reaches to the knees. Its lower border is cut into long, thin strips, to which ornaments are affixed." They often cover the upper parts of their bodies with a light fur which is stitched together at the top. Sometimes it is artfully sewn from small furs of squirrels, field mice, and such.

Nowadays both sexes often use American wool blankets instead of furs. They do not have head ornaments, but instead they hang

Decline and Fall: The American Invasion » 141

about the neck long, rich pendants, including a flat piece of bone which the fair ones use to scrape perspiration from their faces." Rings made of thick brass wire or woven strings with glass beads are worn on the arm joints and legs. They hang small bells or thimbles (brass colored, but not white), in the form of amulets, as ornaments around the neck or attach them to the strips of the skirt. They also decorate the children in this way. As a medium of exchange they use long, white, hollow seashells, from one to two inches long, which come from the north coast of Oregon. They are of the small elephant-tooth type (dentalium) and are placed on strings and worn around the neck. The value of these pieces depends on the length of the shell; thus a shell at least two inches long is worth a dollar. This medium of exchange circulates in the whole coastal area from Russian territory to San Francisco and is thus much in demand by white merchants, because it is accepted as a money substitute by the Indians.

The boys go without clothing during the summer; in the winter they wear small furs. The girls wear leather skirts from the time they are two years old. The faces of the [female] children are tattooed early and in the following manner: three broad stripes are drawn from the mouth to the chin in blue color. The leaders draw snakes or the like on both sides of the chest, on the arms, etc. (See Appendix, 3.).

Everything happens quickly in America and the loss of value of the Indian trade objects, at first highly prized, was rapid. This is due to the wasteful practices of the whites. These cheap things were not highly valued and the Indian is smart enough to recognize, by what he hears or through trade, how little value these things have. Small glass beads, red or white in color and of the size of a small pea, were worth so much in 1850 that for the number contained in a tablespoon one could trade several salmon, several arrows, or objects of the value of about one dollar. For a salmon hook one readily got a fifteen-pound salmon or for four hooks one dollar. A piece of brass wire, the length of a span (about eight inches) for an arm ring cost one to one and a half dollars, thimbles were ten cents apiece, and very small bells were three for a dollar. Needles, thread, scissors, knives, small mirrors, cinnabar for rouge were also wanted but each new article was soon overstocked and its value dropped to almost nothing in their eyes. Old files, which can be forged into long, two-edged knives, also small files, small handaxes, wool blankets, colored silk handkerchiefs (which they tied around their heads or hung on their persons) are still regarded highly because they are expensive. The vanity of the Indian women is apparently innate; they like to look at themselves in the mirror and, whenever they passed my house, they could not resist looking into a piece of mirror fixed to the pump post. Nothing was more amusing though than the fashion in which they wore used womens' clothes which had been given them. One of them appeared in an outer skirt which was much too large, another in a petticoat, and a third one wore simply an apron or a woman's hat with a veil and an Indian skirt,... otherwise walking proudly in her costume of nature. But the men also should be mentioned with regard to vanity. If the government wanted to win the confidence of a leader, thank him, or make more certain of his services, he would be presented with a brightly colored, fantastic uniform, including a military hat, epaulettes, etc. An Indian imagined himself to be a demigod if he wore the cast-off jacket of a soldier (See Appendix, 4.).

One tribe consists of several villages, varying in size and consisting of ten to two hundred families. The area which they consider their home or district is about fifteen to fifty square miles. They seldom come into contact with other tribes except those in the immediate vicinity and with them they trade and also arrange marriages. Their knowledge of other tribes is limited. But in spite of this they get news of the doings of their people and of other important happenings by confidential agents or by sending couriers from tribe to tribe. These couriers can cover long distances in an amazingly short time by short routes known only to themselves. Thus, even in isolated places the Indians are constantly informed of all that happens. This system helps the dispersed Indians in troubles with the whites. In serious quarrels between single tribes, they appear armed and stand facing each other at a distance of fifty paces; women and children stand near by as interested observers.

Decline and Fall: The American Invasion

The chiefs step forward and make long, fiery speeches of defence. If the argument gets hotter, then a few other important men join in; the women cannot be restrained from participating and increase the uproar with loud tongue-lashing. Each side is keyed up for taking up the feud and they are ready to use weapons at the first signal. Recently, fights among themselves have become rare since they have a common, more dangerous enemy, the white man, in the country.

Once our Indian chief pleased me with the presentation of a war chant and dance, performed by a group of ornamented and armed warriors. They lined up in a row with the chief at one end and started a short-syllable uneven yell of even beat. While standing in place, they lifted their feet in a running motion and placed an arrow in their bows. After about two minutes the leader leaped forward for several paces with a savage yell, which the warriors joined with zest, and all shot off their arrows at an angle into the air. This scene started at once over again and was repeated several times (Appendix, 5.)

Each tribe has, besides its regular home, huts in other places to which they move at certain times of the year to make food-gathering easier; for instance, at such suitable places as the estuaries of rivers, at the time of year that the salmon come in, on the coast when salmon fishing is good, and further inland where oak trees are found, at the time the acorns are ripe. Then all families, old and young, with all they have set out, and only very old or sick persons remain at home. From time to time the women bring to the permanent settlements the collected and preserved food in baskets carried on their heads. On trips like this, and always when they travel, the men go first, young men follow, and women and children close the train. Tradition and custom assigns each tribe its own area, in which all gifts of nature belong to that tribe. The population is sparse and infringement on either side does not occur frequently.

Some tribes, living farther inland, live more in holes in the earth than in huts and are called "Digger Indians" by the Americans." Other tribes, like the one described by us, build their dwellings from strong poles joined with clamps. Split boards, two to three feet wide, are placed vertically between these poles as walls. The roof reaches down to three feet from the earth and is made of crosspoles on which boards or planks are placed, and which overlap like shingles, The boards are split from fallen or driftwood pieces or redwood (*Sequoia gigantea*) or other conifers, with wedges made from the antlers of deer and hammers made from traprock or basalt. Boards are made by cutting slits into the logs and prying off the planks with terrific force. A round sliphole, two and a half feet in diameter, serves as an entrance, which can be closed from the inside by a sliding door. The inside of the hut is about four to six feet high in the center, about ten to twenty feet wide, and often dug into the ground for some distance. The cooking fire is kept going in a fireplace, surrounded by stones.[45] This fireplace is in the center of the room. The smoke of the fire escapes through the cracks in the roof and the walls. Weather permitting, a fire is usually kept going outside the hut. They all, old and young, make themselves comfortable in the hut. There are several huts for the food, which is kept in nicely woven baskets.[46] To keep these provisions from spoiling, they must be unpacked from time to time, checked, and the things which are needed, removed. This keeps the women very busy.

In every Indian village there is a building reserved as a sweathouse. The building is sunk all the way into the ground and only the roof with the entrance is visible. In the center of the room is a strong fire, which is fed with dry wood, so that even the walls are quite hot. It is real torture to stay in this room. The old people complain frequently of rheumatism, gout, etc., although their bodies have been conditioned to air and weather changes since childhood. A sweating cure and a cold bath may be just the thing for this, but these people consider sweating a cure for all ills (Appendix, 6.)

Although polygamy seems to be the vogue, many men have only one wife. The leaders and their relatives always have several. Our old chief (he was fifty or sixty years old) had five. The wives are bought from the family and the trade is made with shell money or other valuable objects. The amount of payment varies with the

Decline and Fall: The American Invasion » 145

value of the woman, two or three strings of shells the length of an arm. A woman gains the position of favorite by diligence and aptitude, but all women get along well with each other. The man chooses one or the other alternately to accompany him on his trips. The favorite wife is in charge of keeping and preparing the food, which the head chief distributes to the numerous members of the family near and far. He also has the job of distribution of the catch of fishing or sea hunting, when several families take part in the hunt.

The young people marry early, boys at seventeen to nineteen, and girls at fourteen or fifteen. There are also marriages of elderly people. Widows do not marry again; they wear their hair short as a sign of widowhood."[47]

The women carry the smallest children on trips. The babies sit in light baskets shaped like a deep trough.[48] They are wrapped in furs and strapped in, their legs hanging free. The baskets are carried on the back by means of a carrying band over the forehead. The child in the basket faces toward the rear. The next larger child is led by the hand, and in the other hand the woman holds a long stick as a support. The man or the other women and grown children carry the luggage, etc. (See Appendix, 7.)

Whites, pining for a home, buy themselves Indian wives because of the lack of white women, but the Indian women show themselves to be poorer housewives than with Indian men, where they are forced to work diligently. The main objection the white husband has is the constant presence of the relatives of the woman. These people become true parasites. It seems to be contrary to custom to object to this invasion.

The moving about of single Indian families to visit relatives or neighboring tribes is very frequent. It actually costs the host little, because the entertainment is very easy and is done with food costing nothing while the guests often help with the supplying of food.

Since the Indians do no farming, they have much time for themselves. They use this time to make equipment, weapons, fishing gear, clothing, and boats. The women collect edible plants, which they roast or cook. They cook an onionlike, small bulb, a sea tang, which they form into cakes and bake in the sun. This is eaten instead of bread. They cook large sweet acorns and make mush of them and also cook the husk and the stems of certain slimy tasting plants. The women make flat baskets and caps, from grass, rushes, or small twigs of hazelnut and dry or smoke the supplies of meat and fish. Before the Indians got metal dishes from the whites, they cooked many foods in wooden dishes by throwing hot stones into them. A troublesome work for the women is the collection of firewood. (See Appendix, 8).

Although the needs of the Indians and the industries connected with these needs are not extensive, the Indians show much aptitude and diligence in all types of work and can make many useful things out of raw materials. The twisted strings which they use for fishlines and nets are made from a type of grass and are more durable than our hemplines.[40] They first prepare each cord by rolling it on their thighs and then they combine the twisted cords by letting them run together into a string. This is a truly tedious job. It is interesting to note that all strings of this type made by all Indians from Panama to Oregon are made in the same way and of similar materials.

The bows are made of seasoned wood of the trunk of young *Taxus* or yew trees. This tree does not grow near the coast. The outer side of the two-and-one-fourth-foot bow is covered by narrow bands of stag tendon to give it more strength. The bow is painted with water color and a piece of soft leather covers the place where the arrow is placed. The ends of the bow have short, narrow, notched points, which are bent upward. The bowstrings have loops at each end, which are slipped into the notches of the bowtips. When the bow is not in use, one end of the string is released. Bowstrings are also made from the ankle tendon of the stag.

The arrows are made of light, firm, pithy wood, the thickness of the rib of a swan feather. They are narrow toward the point and have a notch in the other end for the bowstring. Three pieces of feather are tied to the back end with fine tendons to achieve an even flight. The Indians now use thin points of metal for arrowpoints but more often employ splinters of stone, topaz, flint, or the

Decline and Fall: The American Invasion » 147

like. Now they also use bits of broken glass bottles. The iron points probably came earlier through trade from Oregon or Vancouver Island.

The preparation of the stone points is as sensible and practical as it is delicate. A splinter of topaz of suitable size and thickness is held in a thin piece of leather between the fingers of the left hand. Then, by means of the basal edge (the edge nearer the grain) of a dull, rectangular piece of stag horn, one-fourth inch thick, small pieces are pushed or pried off. Here the skill is to produce two fixed barbs and two notches on the edge. A small cleft is cut out in the wood at the end of the arrow. The point sits in this depression. It is then tied to the arrow with fine threads of tendons. Wounds made by these sawlike arrowheads do not heal easily. To make deep body wounds still more dangerous, the Indians make an arrow the tip of which is affixed to a short, thin piece of wood, which is stuck into a hole in the actual arrow.[50] When the arrow is pulled out of the wound, the tip remains in the body. Since these people practice with bows from boyhood on in games, they attain great accuracy when shooting with a fully pulled bow, a feat which is difficult for a white man. The bows and arrows have to be kept as dry as possible because of the use of tendons. Therefore the Indians protect these objects in quivers made of lynx, otter, fox, or marten fur. These animals are skinned without splitting the belly, and the quiver is made in such a way that the hair is turned inward. When it rains, the Indians wrap the quiver carefully in blankets.

They make different tools by grinding, pounding, chipping, breaking, etc. The tools are used for forging, hammering, etc. The perseverance with which they work on a piece of iron, for instance, to make it into a knife has to be admired. They make fishhooks out of fishbones and tips for harpoons out of pieces of bone.

Their construction of canoes is more difficult but very skillful. For this, a piece of the trunk of a fallen, but healthy and completely dry, redwood tree (*Sequoia gigantea*) is taken because it is light weight, easily worked, and lasts well in water. Only half of the trunk is used, the heart making the floor, the outside the freeboards. A trunk five feet in diameter is made into a canoe three and one half feet wide. Fire is used instead of hewing and carving. The burning of the cavities and curves is carefully controlled, and the charred areas are chipped out with sharp stones. This work goes on for months and would do honor to any good carpenter with the best of tools, assuring that a canoe of this sort will last a lifetime. The Indians thus are very careful of the upkeep of the canoes and protect them from the sun by filling them with green branches and leaves. A canoe is turned over when it is not in use and covered with branches. If it begins to leak in spite of this, the Indians try to keep it in shape by tying it together at the ends with spruce or willow branches. The sides of the canoe vary in thickness, according to the size of the craft. They are from one to three inches thick, the bottom and the ends being thicker. The paddles are lancet- or spatula-shaped and about five feet long. A man paddles the canoe either standing or sitting, using both hands and bending the upper part of the body. These canoes are not safe in rough seas and the smaller narrower ones capsize easily. They do not spring leaks readily because of collisions or the effect of water or air. The outer form of the boats is smooth and elegant, nicely rounded in profile. The bow and the stern are decorated by carvings. The boat is usually five to six times as long as it is wide and two thirds as high as wide. (Appendix, 9.)

The hairy furs which they use for clothing are carefully separated from the flesh on the inside and are made pliable by rubbing and kneading. Skins without hair are made into buckskin. The Indians artfully sew together the small furs of squirrels, certain types of hamsters, etc., without our sewing needles or thread.

Since the arrival of the white man the Indians have obtained various new tools and instruments and have quickly learned their use. With these they now do their work more easily and quickly, with great skill, and some of these tools have become indispensable, especially in the preparation of clothing and food, in which these tools have become almost a necessity. For this reason, however, the Indians have become very dependent, since they cannot make these things themselves and the merchant demands money for them. They hire themselves out in order to get money, but they are smart

Decline and Fall: The American Invasion

enough to take advantage of the lack of help and ask high wages. The white man also tries to keep the advantage in any way he can, a condition which is not good for either side. The sad results are apparent in the increase of immorality among the Indians because they could get money without work. Even if only a small number of them have degenerated in this way, the morals of the better ones seem endangered in proportion to the disadvantages they suffer.

When I used some Indians for work for the first time, I did not know what I should give them to eat, since they refused all dishes to which salt, fat, onions, etc., had been added in the kitchen. They also avoided butter and milk but liked fruit, turnips, carrots, etc. They eat meat and fish only if it has been roasted on coals over an open fire. I soon learned their taste and was glad to serve, as the least costly, dishes of which they could eat large quantities. The meals consisted of cooked potatoes, brown sugar instead of salt, hardtack (ship's bread) or white bread, cooked rice with syrup, beans cooked in water, and always black coffee which they loved, probably because of the sugar. Each had to be given his own ration, as I found out to my sorrow, because one of them would take every bit of something he liked away from another. Thus one had to divide the food very carefully. Also, if one gave something to a visiting Indian, all of the people with him demanded the same thing; they are real beggars and, moreover, very sensitive. At first my good housewife often distributed bread or sugar as presents, because of interest; I would have needed a sugar plantation and a mill to satisfy the increasing visits and since they could earn enough money anywhere, I stopped this giving away to adults. When they saw that it did not work, they were satisfied. I can only compare them to children.

Now, more than earlier, they neglect gathering wild plants and use a great deal of wheat flour, hardtack, sugar, or molasses. Let me say to their honor that all of them showed a distaste for alcoholic beverages, although the bad example and offering of the whites was present every day. I knew one worthless young man who liked the taste of fire-water (*metz-papa*) but because of that the others have cast him out.

Another habit, not shared by all of them, is smoking, for which they use the native tobacco plant; it is low-growing, only a foot high, and has white leaves. This smells different from that of the West Indian tobacco plant. In the north they make small, well-made pipes out of basalt; elsewhere, like our Indians, they use a long, straight cigar-holder, of hard wood. They stuff tobacco into the hollow tube, and, tipping the pipe upward, smoke in long drags. For chewing they use a root the size of a small potato, with many strong side roots that have the color and texture of licorice root, with a tart, aniselike taste (Appendix, 10.)

Besides having ability in handicraft, the Indians have ready minds and quickly understand anything that is explained to them. Thus I explained to them, with the aid of a small globe, the position of land and sea where various peoples they knew lived; I explained how the earth moves about the sun and how thus day and night change and, finally, the reason for the lunar eclipse which occurred at that time. As soon as the smart ones understood one sentence, they explained what they had heard to the rest in their own language. I was sorry that I did not know their language well enough; it is very difficult to pronounce and is spoken fluently only by those whites who have Indian wives.[51] There are many consonants in their language, with many guttural and hissing sounds which are difficult to imitate. The Indians often lengthen single syllables and then again speak very rapidly. They often talk in a very low voice, holding the breath. In story-telling, etc., the listener follows the story attentively, repeating the end of each sentence as a sign of understanding.

The young people are attentive, quick, and obedient to their elders; I have never observed corporal punishment.[52] They are gay and uninhibited, and get along with each other in water sports, in races, wrestling, dice, etc. It would be well worth while to devote some care to these young people, still sensitive and pliable. Some boys and girls made very good faithful houseservants. An early removal from a bad environment, and kind but firm treatment is advisable.

I noticed that there existed among them great differences in language and even more important differences in dialect, to such

Decline and Fall: The American Invasion

an extent, in fact, that Indians living about sixty English miles from each other had difficulty in understanding each other, and even those living much nearer each other have many different words. Of course they do not have any words for new things and often use English words for these. The difficulty the Anglo-Saxon has in learning foreign languages soon made it necessary for the Indians to learn English. They have recently started to use many words, although without corresponding sentence structure. We did the same with their language; grimaces and signs were of great help. In this the Indians are very adept, making themselves easily understood:

Here are some words of our tribe:[53]

Aya-que!	Greetings!	Papus	child
Mowema	creator, chief, master, leader	Zik	money
Aloque	Indians	Schlekwa	shirt
Woake	white man	Zallisch	knife
Paha	water	Perscha	gun
Marazza	river	Schmarta	bow
Tep-ha	tree	Winschok	woman
Papschu	bread	Omaha	bad spirit
Mowitsch	stag	Nek	I [first person]
Musch-musch	cattle	Kell	you
Niquitsch	bear	Wokkasan	this or that
Zischi	mule	Lä-ya	way, distance
Nepa	salmon	Skuja	good
Etschque	sea lion	Skenna	small
Tepsi	sea cow	Tenna	large
Squokatsch	seal	Kitzmagay	perished, dead
Nidin	to see	Tscho-ohma!	let's go!
Makamak	to eat	Meruta	five
Merutamak	ten, etc. (See Appendix, 11.)		

I was visited once by a friend, a zither virtuoso from Bavaria. I called several Indians and was interested to note what kind of an impression the instrument would make on them. They listened attentively, enjoyed it, but did not show any special interest or feeling.

Their songs are short and jerky but well timed, and rendered in a monotonous humming, intentionally tremulo. They use few intervals and are rather sad than gay. The women usually hum.

They have an idea of a higher being above them, but I was not able to find an actual cult (See Appendix, 12.)

They bury the dead near their huts and erect a high, close hedge around the grave. Sometimes the grave is covered with large wide, split boards, like a strong chest, in order to keep wild animals away. The mourners tie bunches of feathers of large birds of prey to the tips of the fence. Above the grave, on ropes running the length of the graves are tied some of the clothing, the weapons, and ornaments of the departed. The women mourn for the dead for several days, squatting near the grave, crying and singing in a sobbing voice.[54] (See Appendix, 13.)

I once met an old widow sitting by the grave of her only son, who had been killed in wanton arrogance by a rough Irishman as the young man passed harmlessly by; he had just been buried the day before by his sorrowing tribesmen. I can assure you that what I saw and the circumstances of the case impressed me deeply they will always remain in my mind. I would like to have put a bullet through the head of that unscrupulous murderer. Poor Indians, who have to see such deeds done by whites and almost never find justice or protection, what kind of an impression must you get of the white race and how can it ever expect respect from you? In like arrogance, because of blind suspicion that an Indian was an accomplice in the burning of an empty, miserable wood hut, this same Irishman shot a native, whom we knew, through the shoulders and forearm in such a manner that the Indian was crippled for life and could not work. But neither the Indian nor his relatives took revenge for this, although revenge would have been easy and without discovery on the wooded paths. Revenge would have brought only greater unhappiness to all. I relate these cases because they prove that in many places the whites, on the assumption that they are the stronger, indulge in the commission of the most brutal crimes against the natives. If these crimes become known to other tribes where the injured Indian has blood relatives, and especially if crimes are committed against women, it is no wonder that reprisals are made on travelers. Then the whites complain of the savagery of the Indians and of the danger, and call for military protection. In any case, the whites undertake raids of their own, burn and destroy supplies, and slaughter, with superior weapons, without regard to sex and age, all who do not flee in time, thus teaching the Indians who are clever enough to get away a bad lesson, a lesson which makes them more bitter. Thus it is and thus it will remain as long as brutality and arrogance rule the whites in their relations with the Indians and as long as the established law disregards the punishment of these crimes!

The more he has the opportunity to get to know the good character of the California Indians who have not been aroused to vengeance by their injuries, the more will the just person be interested in their fate. No Indian or tribe will object to just punishment of the true criminal for an unprovoked crime or will protect him—indeed they will help to punish him; but it is difficult to recognize the truth in the labyrinth of wrongdoing on both sides. Here and there it has occurred that Indians, in remote places where they were in the majority, regarded the animals of the miners and settlers as wild game because these animals wandered far afield. Then the Indians ate them. Often, however, these animals were stolen by Mexicans or Chileños or other trash and suspicion fell on the Indians. A mule often cost the life of several human beings and this was the beginning of long hostility. I remember that once it looked very bad for the whites on the Trinity River because the courageous Indians had guns. An Indian agent quieted their anger and was able to get the Indians to surrender their arms into his hands after he promised on his honor that they would be returned after peace had been settled. After both parties had settled down the Indians asked for their guns but the agent refused. The feeling of the savages became violent and the agent returned the guns, but only after they had been made unusable.[65] The Indians then draw their own rules for other occasions from similar bitter experiences. Breach of promise toward colored people and shameless deception are permitted and considered "smart." It is no wonder if now an Indian seldom does anything without having to be shown his reward, be it money or goods. Mistrust is justified and since they have learned overcharging and deduction from wages from the whites, they are beginning to make ridiculously exorbitant demands.

I had a lot to do with our Indian tribe and only once had to complain about the theft of a hunting knife, and that was taken by a strange Indian, although all sorts of equipment and food was easily accessible to them. I admit that some tribes may not be too honest with strangers and there is much theft of things that catch the eye, but I am convinced that no Indian of any tribe near which one lives for a certain time and with whom one is familiar will take any object, even though he may beg for it.

Once I spent half a year with my family in San Francisco and left my youngest son, fourteen years old, who until that time had hunted and fished with the Indians, alone in charge of the isolated ranch to protect it in my absence. The boy had to deal not only with our Indians but also Indians traveling by very often and there was much to steal, not to mention the chance for murder and pilfering, especially of the beautiful and valuable weapons. But there was not the slightest reason to complain about a misuse of trust and the Indians showed themselves worthy of the confidence placed in them. I admit I was more afraid of unpleasantness for my son from the whites than from the Indians. The Indians told me openly that in case of trouble they would have asked a neighboring chieftain for help.

It sometimes happened that all of us men were absent from the farm at night and my wife was left alone at the house; then she permitted some Indian women to sleep in the next building and felt completely safe. Trust creates trust. If the members of our tribe were afraid of being attacked by another tribe not friendly to them, they sought shelter on our grounds, where we did not permit any attacks. In the huts built with my permission near the seashore, they were also safe from the frequent attacks of drunken whites on their women. None of these white brutes ever tried to commit there any such deeds of violence as the women had often to suffer at night in their own village near the city. An attack on the home of a resident white man is a completely different thing from one on the home of a *de facto* rightless Indian. Thus the attachment of these Indians to us was very strong and, when I left the area with my family, they took touching leave of us and the old chief cried like a child.

The bodily strength of these Indians is well known. They excel in swimming and diving; in summer the children spend more of the time in the water than on land. The canoes and other boats, with the exception of the whaling boats, do not withstand high waves well. If a canoe capsizes, these people swim out to it, right it or push it in front of them toward the beach. They dive under the highest waves and come up like seals on the other side. They swim with all types of strokes but mostly with alternating strokes like the animals. Even as children they acquire this great physical ability and strength by wrestling, racing, catching, swimming, rowing, etc. They move with remarkable ease through the dense woods. They hop, slide, and climb like apes and one really has to work to keep up with them. They do remarkably well in marching and I often sent Indians to a village fifteen miles away and they made the round trip in ten to twelve hours. As has been mentioned, they carry loads by means of broad carrying ropes woven from strings, which are placed over the forehead. With a quarter of an elk (about one hundred and fifty pounds) on his back the Indian can walk for half a day without interruption over all obstacles, through forests and valleys and over the steepest rises. The women are only a little behind the stronger sex.

They soon learned how to use firearms and I have seen young people shoot fairly well after relatively little practice. Here their interest, their training in hunting, their sharp eyes and steady hands are of help. Their highest goal is to own a rifle but, since the purchase and owning of a rifle is forbidden by law, they keep them hidden.

Hunting and fishing is the main source of food for the redskins. Hunting would be easier with the use of guns. Small animals like deer, foxes, lynx, otters, etc., are easily killed with arrows, but often arrows do not easily kill larger animals like elk or bears, and the hunter is thus often endangered when hunting beasts of prey. For these animals they often set on the runs traps made of rope one and a quarter inches thick[56] or dig pitfalls, which are covered with twigs. For sea hunting there are various large sea animals like sea lions, sea-cows, and especially the abundant seal. The Indians hunt the sea lions with canoes and look for them on isolated rocks in the sea, where the animals like to sleep in the sun. It is always difficult in the moving sea to jump from the boat to the rock. My young son was often asked by the Indians to aid them in the hunt with his gun and thus do them a great favor. I usually permitted this because these animals are important sources of food to them. After they returned to the shore, the game is divided by the chief and distributed to the elders. Then they proceed to smoke the meat, melt the blubber, etc. The oil is kept in the large bladders of these animals and is well liked as a drink.

Salmon fishing takes up all their time during the summer from the beginning of July to the end of September. The fishing is divided into sea and river fishing, and the success is not the same every year. The salmon travel in great schools and their presence near the shore, mostly on the beach in bays, is shown by the many pelicans which dive into the sea and arise again, swallowing their prey. The Indians use small two- or four-man canoes. When they arrive at the fishing place, they first catch a number of baitfish with sardine spears. These are killed and placed on the fishhooks tied to both ends of a long fishline. One hook is thrown out on each side so that each Indian fishes with two hooks. The canoe is left to itself, unless a wind forces them to row to keep it in the proper place; then one of the men in the canoe does this. The salmon is played for some time, according to its size, until it is brought to the side of the boat and beaten to death in the water with a small cudgel. The size of the catch varies and sometimes sixty to one hundred fish are landed in one boat within a few hours, so that it almost sinks. At other times only two to six fish are caught in the same length of time. All fish are properly cleaned after the boat lands. The Indians, especially the women, are very expert at cutting the fish lengthwise into two halves, joined at the tail and along the skin of the backs. Thus the smoking and drying, which is done on stands of vertical sticks, three feet above the ground, is more complete and faster. The Indians use weak, smoky fires in the open, in the shade, or even inside the living quarters.

Sometimes the Indians catch other types of fish with fishhooks from the shore.

It is known that the salmon travels upstream at spawning time. At that time the Indians move to rivers which empty over sandbars into the sea, where the salmon can easily be seen in the shallow water at ebbtide. The fish are brought into the shallow water by the movement of the waves and often miss the true estuary. The Indians, standing at intervals of fifty to eighty feet in the shallow water, quickly spear the fish with a harpoon on a long pole by a quick thrust toward the tail of the fish. Here one has to be very quick because, before one knows it, a wave may carry the fish back into deeper water. The salmon tends to spawn when it is foggy or rainy. In the early spring, when some of the salmon are still on the way back to the sea, they are caught in the upper stretches of the rivers in the following manner: a type of wicker fence is built across the shallows of the stream so that the fish can not swim downstream and collect in the deeper water.[57] They are then killed with spears or pulled out by dragnets. This type of fishing is now prohibited by the government.

In the fall, the Indians in our locality often caught lampreys, salmon trout, and other kinds of fish in the small rivers of the coast.

They do not dare come near to whales with the insufficient equipment they have, although they are very fond of whale blubber and meat. But several times whales were stranded on the flat beach or were washed up dead on the shore. Then our whole Indian population, shouting with joy about the grand gift from heaven, moved to the place and in a few days supplies of meat and blubber had been collected and prepared.

The Indians sometimes caught many crabs near the estuary of the rivers. These crabs were there to change their shells and the Indians speared them in the shallow water with pointed poles. In canoes they collected quantities of various edible mussels from the rocks of the coast. They often brought fish and mussels to the whites for sale but sold them not too cheaply, considering how easy it was to collect them (see Appendix, 14).

It seems to me that it is unfair of the government to consider all land on which the Indians have lived until now the sole property of the United States and the Indians themselves as "tenants." This is done, under the guise of a law, to regulate the presence of the Indians and to permit the whites to take possession of the good land, and also for the purpose of having the Indians live separately from the whites, a purpose achieved by the establishment of the above-mentioned Indian Reservations.

Another injustice is the provision that Indians, like Negroes, cannot lawfully be witnesses, a provision which deprives them of any defence or protection in conflicts with the whites and gives the white man special rights in all cases of unjust practices, and, indeed, sanctions all their crimes."[58] (See Appendix, 15.)

Appendix to Loeffelholz's Account

1. These were, in fact, the Zoreisch [Tsorei] Indians under discussion. These first came in contact with white men around the year 1850, and at that time still used exclusively weapons and tools of stone and bone.[59]

Since the small population (actually only about fifty to eighty people) which lived on the roadstead protected by Trinidad Head got their food chiefly from the sea, most of their simple equipment was for fishing.

Once in a while a sailing ship may have appeared in the blue expanse of the sea, ships which sailed to Astoria (founded in 1820 or so on the Columbia River) for furs. Also the Spaniards and later Behring in 1729 and Cook in 1778 entered these waters.[60] Perhaps the Spaniards or these explorers used the open bay for a short stay, but for these early comers there was little attraction in the virgin forest of sequoia, those giants of California, which grew along the

Decline and Fall: The American Invasion » 159

coast and towered inland as far as the eye could see to the gradual slope of the wooded mountains and which gave no hint of the buried golden treasure of the interior. Nor did they see those grassy plains which offered the indolent Southerner the opportunity to carry on his lazy, half-civilized stock raising. On the steep coast, easily visible from the sea, the explorer saw no places of interest, like bays or estuaries, which could have caused him to stay awhile and investigate.

If a ship ever did sail into the lonely bay, the frightened and superstitious natives would probably have fled from their huts into the bush, as one reads in the accounts of the earlier explorers. The strange appearance of the men who had landed, their use of the wild for hunting, the cracking of the gun which first disturbed the majestic quiet of the giant redwoods, all these would have frightened them even more, so that a meeting with the white men did not occur; at least, there is no trace of any such communication in legends or in native equipment. The distance to the early European settlements and the lack of communication between the small tribes, increased by the difficulty in travel and the intertribal enmities, also explain the fact that the prized and useful European products had not yet reached them.

The rock mountain which forms the bay juts far out into the sea and is connected with the mainland by a narrow isthmus. On this isthmus was built, overnight so to speak, the little coastal town of Trinidad in 1850–1851, from which all mining operations in the interior were provisioned. The coast is a more or less steep, rocky slope, and the Indian village is situated on a small plateau below the south end of the town. Its six to eight huts are each from ten to twelve meters long, not quite as wide, and are irregularly grouped. A huge wild laurel bush of strange growth (its trunk had fallen over some time before and it had become rooted on its side) covers several huts like a great arbor with its far-spreading, shady branches and its deep green foliage.[61] Under it, from a cleft in the slate, runs a profuse spring, which supplied the people with water at an easy distance. To get more water the little stream has been damned.

Between those huts which are a little farther apart are wall-like mounds of mussels, mainly the span-long edible mussel, true Kjökkenmöddinger.[62] These heaps of mussels, whose size indicates the great age of the village, are overgrown, like the surrounding area, with nettles, which in some area have given way to field ferns almost as tall as a man.

2. The Tsorei Indians are of medium height (160–165 cm. or even less). As usual, the women are smaller, of well proportioned build, often slender and broad-shouldered, with small hands and feet. The features are of the familiar Indian type; somewhat prominent cheekbones, a round, almost broad face, well-formed noses, which look Roman in some of them but always with broad flaring nostrils. Their eyes are dark and they have luxuriant, black, sleek hair. Both sexes wear their hair parted and hanging free in back. Often, while hunting or at other occupations where free hair would bother them, they tie the hair in back in a bun, in the manner of the old Germans, or tie it with a band over the forehead. The women often wear their hair in braids on the sides of the head, letting the braids hang down in front over the shoulders. Like all wild people, the hair is infested with lice and the women, especially, spend much time hunting for them. Those which are caught are simply eaten.

The skin color shows varying shades of red-brown, best described as "copper colored." Some boys and girls can be considered good-looking by European standards. The women, however, age very quickly, and after their first children their breasts become pendulous, since they nurse the children for two or three years or even longer.

The men carefully pull out all beard hairs. They do this with tweezers made of mussel shells, still held together at the joint. Only once we saw an Indian, a very old man of a neighboring tribe, who had a sparse, gray beard while the hair on his head was still fresh and black.

3. The women, but seldom the men, beautify themselves by tattooing. But these marks are sparse and simple, consisting of three blue stripes, each the width of a finger, running downward from the corners and the middle of the mouth.

Instead of this, the men often paint their faces and bodies, the figures and the extent of the painting depend on the individual taste. Only the color has any particular meaning. On happy occasions they use red; white is the color of mourning; and black with red is the color of war. The black color has the advantage that on the dark skin it is not easily visible at a distance but looks very horrible near by. The paint patterns usually consist of three horizontal stripes on the cheek, one or two on the forehead, with semicircles or circles around the eyes.

At first one still saw the native dress very often. The men and children go naked, especially around the village and in the huts. At other times the men wear a soft, tanned stag or deer skin with the hair on the outside. The skin is drawn underneath the left shoulder and tied together over the right shoulder so that there is freedom of movement for the arm. The women and also the older girls wear a piece of tanned dehaired elk leather, long enough to be wound around the body two or three times. At a distance of about three inches, a handsbreadth, from the top this is cut into narrow strips, two to three millimeters wide, which reach to the knees. The women often use glass beads to ornament the skirt. These are fixed to the strips or hung on strings between the strips. They also use bast to make these skirts, but only very seldom.

After they became acquainted with wool blankets, men and women wore them frequently in the manner described above or threw them over their backs and held them together with their hands in front. Later on they also used European clothing and sometimes wore them in the funniest combinations. But as rapidly as they take a fancy to a highly grotesque piece of clothing, as quickly they change fashion according to their mood. They like civilized footwear least of all, because they have always gone barefoot, being accustomed from childhood to the temperature, which remains even almost always and only drops to freezing for a few hours. Thus they get on well without warm clothing.

The men often use a band over the forehead to keep the loose hair in place, especially when rowing. The band is half an inch wide and is made out of strings around which colored roots have been woven. The women, less often the men, wear small basket caps as head coverings. These baskets are hemispherical in shape and nicely woven and colored. These, however, are less used for this purpose than for water cups or cooking utensils.

On festive occasions, and always when they go to war, the men place one or more brown feathers of sea eagles in the hair or the headband. At feasts they also use the nice red feathers of the woodpecker. The most treasured possession of the chief is a belt made of otterskin, about thirty-six inches long, on which are sewn the gorgeous purple-red crests of the big black woodpeckers. The belt is kept carefully in the prepared gut of a sea lion. Another ornament which, like the glass beads, appeared only a short time ago with the coming of the whites is the arm and leg rings made of brass wire. This ornament was used mainly by the women.

4. They valued red glass beads the most, then milky white or blue ones, and preferred the small beads. Other colors were less popular and so were the large, multicolored Venetian beads. They regarded yellow beads with definite distaste and refused them, even if one tried to give them away,[68] probably because of superstition. The men did not often wear these ornaments but the women always had several strings of beads hanging around the neck and over the breast; sometimes they also wore strings of beads around their arms or legs. The men decorated their quivers with beads just as the women trimmed their skirts.

The long, conical, cylindrical, porcelainlike shells of the *Aloquezik*, or Indian money as they called it (Dentalium elephantinum), are prized highly as a medium of exchange. These take the place of money, and are also worn as ornaments. These shells, as far as we know, are not found in the sea in this vicinity but came to them through trade with other tribes, though there is no other indication of this trade. The shells are placed on strings and their value is measured according to the length of the forearm. An Indian pays ten to twenty of these strings when he buys a wife. There are probably imitations or less valuable kinds of these shells because the Indians often test them by biting off their ends.

5. The chief as such did not have any definite influence on the members of his tribe. Only as the oldest man was he given some

respect, especially in the more important matters. He was the leader in war, the fighter. Otherwise, every grown man could do what he wanted. The manner of these Indians was always peaceful and well-meaning. They limited themselves to the protection of their homes and near-by fishing and hunting areas against other tribes. With the sparse population and the rich sources of food that the sea offered to the coastal Indians, there was no reason for fighting, as there was for the Indians of the more populated East. There was almost continual war between the Eastern tribes, because they needed such extensive hunting grounds. Here in California for several years there was only one revolt in which blood was spilled. The chief was wounded in the abdomen by an arrow but the wound healed soon with the application of leaves and the use of a bandage. The "criminal" and his family remained away from the village for several months but he then made friends again with his opponent by gifts." The argument had been started by the women, and all during the "fight" there was more noise, shouting, and milling about of the men and women of the whole tribe than an actual battle. The chief, who tried to mediate, got the worst of it, being hit by an arrow during the melee. He could easily have avoided this arrow at a greater distance. The Indians, by a quick movement, are able to avoid flying arrows at a distance of twenty to thirty paces.

There never seemed to be much bloodshed even in the occasional wars made against the neighboring Indian tribe which lived on the Mad River about twenty miles away. Before they set out against the enemy, a war dance, with as much noise and shouting as possible, was held in the village. For this, the army (some ten to twenty men, because it was seldom that all could be brought together or were present in the village) lined up in a single file. The man on the right end was the first dancer and singer. Each man held bow and arrow in his hands. They imitated the shooting of arrows or, by quick bodily movements, imitated dodging the arrows. All of them sang loudly and stamped their feet on the ground so that after the dance the grass showed a dark line like a well-worn path. At the end of the song the wing man leapt forward and shot off his arrow with such force that it disappeared from sight.

6. The huts are made of boards one to one and a half meters wide, three to eight centimeters thick, and three to four meters long, of redwood (*Sequoia gigantea*). This wood is easily worked and resists decay. The walls are vertical boards set into the ground and are about one and a half meters high. Boards of the same type, often a meter in breadth, were used for the roof, slanting down from a strong ridgepole in the middle. The inside of the room was then of a height of three to four meters in the center and one and a half meters at the sides. The peculiar thing was the single entrance, which was on the ridge side of head hut. It was a circular opening, hardly a meter in diameter, in one of the wide planks about a half meter above the ground. It could be closed with a board from the inside. Light and smoke had to find their way through the many cracks between the boards, which did not fit well together.

The hearth was in the center of the room. It was sunk into the ground and was surrounded by several stones. It was only used when the weather was bad; otherwise, the cooking was done in the open. The baskets with the few supplies collected by the Indians for the winter stood in the corners and against the walls. These supplies consisted mostly of smoked salmon, which either in this condition or fresh was their main food. There was also dried meat. A variety of spears for fishing, fishlines, nets, arrows, and bows were kept in quivers on the walls and roof. The bows were carefully protected against moisture.

The floor of the hut was the earth, which could be used as a sleeping place without any special preparation owing to the mild climate, which reached freezing temperatures only rarely at night. A piece of tanned stag leather was used as a bed (later, after they become acquainted with wool blankets they used these to lie on and also for covers), and a piece of wood served for a pillow.

The entrances of the huts faced toward a small "village square" in the center of the village. The shape and size of these openings probably served to facilitate defense against attacks since, even if they were open, the attacker had to crawl on all fours and thus could easily be put out of action by means of a cudgel. Arrows could be shot from the inside through the cracks in the walls and thus the hut became almost a fortress.

At the time of salmon fishing in the summer all able-bodied persons moved to the best fishing place, about an hour's journey south of the village, where they built huts out of alder branches. Here they smoked the fish during the day, the dense foliage protecting them from the cold of the morning and the exceptionally heavy dew. These huts were not always built in the same places but were always in the vicinity of the best place for fishing at that time. The small children and some women stayed in the village to protect it.

They built huts, like those in the village but smaller, at places which were good the year around for obtaining food. The estuary of the Little River was such a place and there, during the rainy season of the winter when most food was needed, they could hunt the salmon coming there to spawn.[65]

They were also acquainted with sweathouses. These were built like the huts but were smaller and sunken all the way into the ground. Even the roof was covered with earth so that the warm air could not escape. For an entrance there was a small hole in the roof, which could be closed with a lid. In the center of the hut there was the fireplace, where a medium-sized fire was kept with thin, very dry alder branches stripped of their bark, which made no smoke. The older Indians often complained of rheumatism and for this they used the sweat bath. They lay down on the floor of the sweathouse and started a song, with which they kept time by hitting a small stone against a larger one or a piece of wood. They soon sweated profusely, owing to the intense heat. Then they ran quickly to the near-by sea and dived in head first. There they swam and dived for a time.

Usually, the fire burned continually in the huts or at the camping places. The live coals in the ashes were fanned into a new fire every morning. The women carried torches or live coals with them when the Indians went on short trips. This was easier than the tedious process of starting a new fire by rubbing two pieces of wood together, a process which required skill and strength and was done by the men. One of the pieces of wood was a soft, dry piece of willow, fifty centimeters long and four centimeters wide, with small pits in it made by stone splinters. A piece of harder wood,[66] looking like the shaft of an arrow but thicker, was placed in one of these pits and was twirled between the palms of the hands as fast as possible. The hands slid down and had to be pulled rapidly upwards again. After some minutes of continuous exertion some glowing dust collected in the pit and the walls of the pit also smoked. A flame then was started by placing fine, dry grass near the sparks and blowing. The apparatus had to be protected from moisture very carefully and was carried in a quiver. Naturally it disappeared soon after the introduction of the European lighter.

Another utensil, already mentioned, was the hemispherical headdress of the women, which was used as a water cup or for cooking. The women made these out of strands split from roots of certain plants; the weave resembled that of Panama hats. These hats were watertight and trimmed with color.

The women also made baskets of different sizes and shapes. These were woven tightly from unpeeled willow branches. These baskets were used to carry and keep the provisions which had been collected. The baskets, like the babies, were carried by the women by means of a woven string belt or band two to three fingers wide, which passed from the load across the forehead. The men carried their hunting booty or other heavy things in the same manner. They often held the band in place next to the head with their hands and could carry fifty to seventy kilograms for half a day without resting.

The Indians kept a few dogs around the village as domestic animals. These usually stayed near the village. The dogs apparently were descendants of the wild dog (coyote) of the country and had long hair; they were of considerable size and resembled the American wolf. Besides the inhabitants of the hair [lice] which have already been mentioned there were a lot of fleas, especially in the deserted huts or campsites.

7. Polygamy was permitted, but a man seldom took several wives and even then he usually lived with only one of them. Even the chief apparently had only two wives and the older one lived apart from him. (The second marriage of Indian males is probably explained by the rapid aging of the women, who marry very young, at fourteen to eighteen years.) A second wife was an expensive luxury,

Decline and Fall: The American Invasion » 167

because the woman had to be bought from her family. According to hearsay, a wife cost forty to eighty dollars or, according to their values, ten to twenty bows, eight to sixteen otterskins, or a rifle. This last, however, could be possessed only secretly, since it was against the law.

The number of children was not large. The chief had one son living (a son by his first wife) and two sons and a daughter by his second wife. Other families had two or three children, mostly boys.

Usually, several families of one tribe lived in one of the larger huts in the village. The father lived with the family of his children. Manner and customs of sexual intercourse seemed to have been the same as those of most of the North American Indian tribes.[67]

8. In the summer the women and children collected raspberries, which grew in great quantities at the edge of the forest. They also collected the berries of the arrowwood and blackberry-like fruits growing in bunches like currants on small leathery-leafed bushes in the open. The young sprouts of the raspberry bush as well as the stems of other plants were peeled and eaten. The women dug up an onionlike bulb the size of a hazel-nut by means of wooden chisels. When baked, the bulb was mealy and sticky and tasted sweet.[68] The oak trees growing further inland in the forest glades gave them acorns, which were kept dried and were made into flour by rubbing them between stones. This flour was mixed with water in the head baskets and heated with hot stones to make a mushlike dish. They ate *Aloque-papschu* more often than the foregoing dishes. The Indian bread, as they called it, was made from the small, thin leaves of a seaweed which grew on the rocks of the coast. It was simply dried in the sun and eaten without further preparation.

They knew only water and fish oil for drinking. The latter was used only seldom as a drink; it was also used for rubbing on the body. They did not like the "firewater" of the whites at first; only after some years one or the other drank some and then not much. On the other hand, they liked the food of the white man very much and traded or begged for it. They especially liked biscuit, sugar, and flour, which they baked into bread in the ashes, as the miners did.

Fish, small game, and pieces of meat were placed on live coals or on small wooden spits near the fire. Larger pieces of meat were roasted in the usual way in heated pits in the ground.

The Tsorei Indians were a friendly, well-meaning people, who probably lived a quiet and carefree life in the idyllic loneliness of the village for hundreds of years, protected from any serious food shortages by the sea. They went away only from time to time to hunt and fish, but never went more than twenty kilometers from their village. They would probably have trespassed on the land of another tribe, had they gone further. There seems to have been a boundary and a mutual agreement between them because, even at the time for salmon fishing, one could see only a few members of the northern tribes. These persons were probably related by marriage or had been invited. The character of the Indians was honest and frank. They seldom fought among themselves, and such a fight was quickly settled. They rewarded good treatment with trust and attachment.

In the relations between the sexes they were moral, although the nakedness of the men in earlier times and the custom of offering the wife to a guest does not conform to European views.

9. The bow and arrow was their main weapon for war and hunting. The arrow had a stone tip, although within half a year after they became acquainted with bottle glass and iron they used these for arrowheads.

Only since their meeting with the white man have they used a different, hitherto unknown weapon or piece of equipment. This was a symmetrically tapered, two-edged sword about sixty centimeters long and five to eight centimeters wide, which they made from pieces of old steel woodsaws or from pieces of iron obtained in trade and filed them into the desired shape. It had a handle made from stag antlers. These swords were carried without a sheath, hanging from the shoulder on a cord or sometimes with the arrows in the quiver. It is remarkable that they independently manufactured a sword of this kind, although they had no such model, but had seen instead bowies, machetes, and other modern weapons and equipment made from metal.[60]

The great importance which fishing held in their lives was indi-

Decline and Fall: The American Invasion » 169

cated by the variety of fishing equipment, and they showed great inventiveness in its manufacture and use. They made good fishlines and nets out of the brown, thin plant fiber, about half a meter long. Working with the palms of their hands on their naked thighs they twisted two of these fibers together, one clockwise and the other counterclockwise, to prevent unraveling in the water. The lines were up to seven millimeters in diameter and were superior in quality to the best hemplines.

The spear used to spear the salmon was a redwood pole six meters long and about four centimeters in diameter, with a short conical piece of hardwood tied firmly to its top. To this piece of wood they fastened a point made of a flat piece of stag horn with sharply ground edges and with two barbs at the base.[70] This was bound to the line by a closely wound string of tendon and glued tight with pine resin. The other end of the line, one and a half meters long, was fastened to the pole. When a fish was speared, the point came loose from the shaft, which would have been broken by the violent struggling of the fish if the line had been taut. The line prevented the fish from freeing itself.

The sardines used as bait were caught from the canoe by means of a spear which had a similar shaft. At the end of the shaft there were about twenty small, pointed hardwood sticks about twenty centimeters in length. These thin, flexible sticks were fastened in such a way that they were separated at the end. This spear was pushed vertically into the sea into a school of sardines and each time a number of the little fishes were caught between the sticks or speared on them.

The tribe had about five or six canoes for hunting and fishing in the sea. The chief owned the biggest canoe. It was about eight or nine meters long, one and a half meters wide, and about seventy centimeters deep. It was turned up at the bow and stern and had rounded, slightly elevated sides and a rounded body. The cross section of the canoe was almost a semicircle at the center. The bottom was somewhat flattened. The sides of the canoe were five to eight centimeters thick and had strips of wood at the upper edge. These strips were bent inward to make handling the boat easier when it was launched or pulled back onto the land. The canoes were made exclusively of redwood, which is soft but resists rotting and cracking well, and is easy to work on. This was imperative since they had neither stone axes nor chisels. All they had for the construction of canoes was a chisel made from stag horn, and fire. They used redwood paddles about two meters long, with blades shaped like willow leaves. They paddled with both hands, standing, sitting, or kneeling.

The bow of the Tsorei Indians was small, barely a meter long, about five centimeters wide in the middle and two centimeters thick. It was slightly arched toward the outside, was flat on the inside, tapering towards the almost cylindrical ends, which were bent up a little. The bow was made of a stiff redwood bough and covered on the outside with a very thin layer of fresh deer sinew, which was tied to the wood and lasted a long time. This cover had to be protected against humidity, which would soften and loosen the sinew.

During the spreading and drying of this cover, the wood was stretched in the direction opposite its final bend. This position was always assumed by the bow when the bowstring was not hooked in and had to be overcome by a strong pressure at the center when one fixed the bowstring. Thus the bow always had great power despite its short length and pull. The string was a stag tendon, three millimeters in diameter, which had been twisted together like a rope. It had loops on both ends and these loops were pushed over the bent ends of the bow. The string was always removed from one end of the bow if the bow was not being used for some time, and the released bow was kept in the quiver. The strength and pliability of the bow was so great that, thanks to the sinew covering, one could bend it into a semicircle by pulling it with the whole hand (a pull of 50–75 kg.) and yet it would not break.[11] The pull used for shooting was not that great, because for this the bowstring was grasped with the thumb and forefinger on the arrow.

They made arrows out of the straight shoots of the above-mentioned redberry bush. The arrows were seventy-five to eighty-five centimeters long and seven and nine millimeters thick. The diameter decreased a little toward one end. There was a small notch in

Decline and Fall: The American Invasion » 171

the lower end of the arrow for the bowstring, and also three hawk or falcon feathers, split lengthwise, were attached at this end. The feathers, about ten centimeters long, with trimmed edges, were tied at their ends to the shaft with thin strips of tendon. Narrow, colored rings on the lower part of the shaft served as decorations or marks, which distinguished the arrows in the quiver. There were hunting arrows, which had a broad red band, and war arrows with a black band. The war arrows also had fine cuts on the shaft to permit a better finger grip. These cuts were made with a sharp stone splinter, one man holding the chisel while another turned the arrow quickly between the palms of his hands. These stone splinters were also used for scraping, cutting, and sawing. The material being worked on was held between the teeth or with the big toes. The big toes thus had great strength and agility.

The stone points of the hunting arrows (later also the glass and iron tips) rested in a groove on the end of the shaft and were attached with thin tendon fibres to grooves in the shaft and glued there with resin. The points of the war arrows, on the other hand, were fixed to sticks a handsbreadth long (as described above), which fitted into a conical hollow in the upper end of the shaft. This upper part of the shaft was wound with tendon to prevent splitting. This construction permitted the stone point and the stick to remain in the wound when the arrow was pulled out.

The stone arrowpoints were beautiful and artistic; they were made with sharp, sawtoothed cutting tools from flakes of different silica or semiprecious stones. There was no flint in the locality. Small flakes were pried loose from the edges of the siliceous splinters by means of a quadrangular piece of stag horn. The big flake was tied to a stick about fifty centimeters long to permit better handling. The end of this stick was held close to the body by the upper arm and the prying was done with the piece of stag horn held in one hand. The stone tip was held in a piece of deerskin between the thumb and the index finger of the left hand and thus could be twisted and turned. Later on they liked to use green bottle-glass, which could be chipped more easily and could be made more quickly into arrowpoints. They also prepared metal points from barrel hoops, etc. They shaped these by means of three-sided saw files and fixed them with long barbs.

One bow and from ten to thirty arrows were kept in a quiver. The quiver was covered by animal skin with the hair turned inward and was carried on a string over the left shoulder. The skin of the fish otter was preferred as a quiver cover and a quiver of this kind was more valuable. The Indians knew how to tan skins well, with or without the hair. They used fish oil or lime from burned shells for this purpose and scraped the skin with sharp stone splinters.

When hunting big game, the hunter often placed two or three arrows in the bow at the same time, holding them ready with the left hand while one arrow was shot. Thus three arrows could be shot off in the space of a few seconds.

They had special spears which they used to hunt sea lions, seals, or other animals of this kind. The point of these spears was a long flat piece of stag horn, three centimeters wide, which had two strong barbs on one side. At its end there was the actual tip, a flaked stone tip resting in a hollow and glued tight with resin. At its lower end the harpoon had a protuberance with a square end. By means of this the harpoon head could easily be set into a recess in the end of the shaft. A strong line (about eight mm. thick) was attached to one side of the horn point and was wound around the shaft so it could be unwound easily. If a seal was wounded by an arrow or a gunshot, it received a much more serious wound with a thrust of the spear. (If the animal died, it sank to the bottom and was often lost to the hunter.) The tip was held fast in the animal because of the barbs, and the detached from the shaft. If the animal sank, the line (about thirty meters long) unwound and the floating shaft showed the location of the animal. The shaft was about two meters long, cylindrical at the tip end, and flat at the other.

The Tsorei Indians needed only a few real tools for their work. Wedges and chisels from the huge antlers of the large elk (the size of a horse) were polished with sandstone and were used in the building of canoes and for hacking and splitting the thick planks for houses and graves. Huge trunks of the *Sequoia* lay everywhere after they had drifted onto the beach. These tree trunks were used

Decline and Fall: The American Invasion » 173

for building. The Indians cut slits crosswise into the trunks with a chisel, using a boulder as a mallet. When the cuts were deep enough, according to the thickness of the board, the wood was pried off by means of such chisels and wedges. This was easy because the redwood was soft and fine-grained.

Sharpened stones and sharp stone splinters were used to prepare the horn and bone parts of the spears. They were also used for scraping and turning arrows, tanning furs, and skinning and cutting up game. They did not have polished stone weapons or tools.[72]

10. The men indulged in the old, widely known Indian custom of smoking. They smoked seldom, only once or twice a month. The dried, green leaves of a hemplike plant, which did not grow near the coast, were used as tobacco. They crumbled the leaves by rubbing them between the hands and then placed them in a simple, funnel-shaped hollow in an elderberry stalk. The smoker's head was thrown back and the smoke was inhaled by deep drags and expelled through the nose.

11. Some words of the Tsorei Indians are given and, as a comparison, the same words of the Tlinkits of Alaska (from Dr. A. Krause).[73]

English	Tsorei	English	Tsorei
tree	tepāh	salmon	nepa
fire	metz	Indian	aloque
water	paha	White	woake
bear	niquitsch	money	zik
sea lion	etschque	Indian-money (Dentalium)	aloque-zik
sea cow	tepsi	money of whites	woake-zik
seal	squokatsch	woman	wintschok
gun	persha	bad spirit (wood)	umaha
bow	smarda	Little River	skena-maraz
knife	zalisch	Trinidad Indian	Tsorei (aloque)

English	Tsorei	English	Tsorei
small	skena	Mad River Indian	walawala
large	denna	cussword	woschaa
chief	mowema	dead, die	kitzmakei
God	denna mowema	hair	leptag
none, not	peiowah	speak	wauwau
yes	eh	Let's go!	Zoho umo!
no	päh	fish otter	schräz
good	skuja	cord	pakzes
bad	kumalo	bush	gäb
very far	denna läjo	I	nek
go	zoho	you	kel
one	spini	see	nidin
ten	merutamak	hand	slekwa
bread	papschu	hungry	ziawe
wild duck	lakak	eat	mukamuk

Common Signs[74]

To be married: both index fingers, bent, are hooked into each other. Brother and sister: both index fingers are extended straight out, side by side. Insult: the five fingers of a hand are extended against that person. Anihilation (in war): rubbing together of thumb and index finger. The words papus (child), squaw (woman), and canoe were probably learned and taken over from the white population.

12. They had general ideas of good and bad, which they heeded. Their religion, if one may call these confused, obscure concepts religion, was also simple. A great spirit, *denna-mowema* (the great chief or lord) ruled them all; the soul lived after death. A bad spirit, *umaha,* lived in the huge forest; they sometimes attempted to scare it away at night from their camp in the forest by yelling and torches. Spirits were also supposed to live in the caves of the coastal rocks:[75] If the Indians passed by one in a canoe, the chief or the oldest man started a song.

13. Their dead were usually buried near the place of death at the village, in shrubbery a few hundred paces away on the slope or near the edge of the forest. The corpse was stretched out in a grave one to one and a half meters deep and covered with earth.[76] On the earth was placed a wide redwood plank; then more earth, another plank, earth, and finally a third plank on the top. The planks were probably used only to prevent wild animals from digging up the corpse. The women, sitting around the body, sang laments before the dead was buried. Later on they avoided the grave and seemed frightened and revolted when they saw a skeleton. The men painted themselves with white clay for a time as a sign of mourning.

14. The sea was their main source of food. This supply was never spoiled or exhausted, something which could easily happen with the fleet game of the forest. If one classifies a people according to the old division into hunters, fishers, herders, or farmers, one would be correct in counting the Tsorei Indians as fishers, since their most important food was fish, especially the sea salmon. They even stored fish for the winter.

Huge schools of sardines usually appeared in the vicinity of the coast in the middle of June and with them came the salmon. Canoes were used for fishing. First a number of sardines were caught for bait. A dead fish was hooked through its back on an iron fishhook (soon after the arrival of the white man these had replaced the earlier hooks made of horn or the like) and the lines were thrown in without a sinker. Each fisherman handled a line on the right and on the left side. A usual average daily catch of one canoe was about five to twenty salmon. It sometimes happened, however, that in good times and at suitable places within an hour a canoe was loaded almost to sinking with sixty to one hundred salmon weighing five to twenty-five kilograms. The fishing season lasted four to six weeks. Then the huge schools of sardines, and with them the salmon, disappeared as suddenly as they had appeared.

The salmon, after several months' absence, appeared again on the coast at the beginning of December, when the rainy season started. It is not certain whether this was the same species, because instead of the nicely formed head of the summer salmon, the thick, ugly upper jaw of this species was lengthened and bent downward with a sort of proboscis. The scales no longer had the silvery sheen and the meat was not a nice rosy red but paler. The female carried a lot of eggs by this time and the eggs were almost the size of peas, The fish now entered the estuaries of the rivers to go upstream.

The Little River pours into the sea over a barrier and the breakers of the sea run far up the flat sandy beach and then retreat. Here the fish look for the estuary of the river and swim around in the shallow water off the beach. Here the presence of the fish is indicated by the ripples made on the smooth surface. In this kind of fishing, several Indians stand at a distance of fifty to one hundred paces from each other knee-deep in the water. As soon as one of them sees the trace of a salmon he runs toward it and stabs with his spear at the fish, thrusting the weapon flat along the surface of the water or throwing it with considerable strength and piercing the fish with the horn tip. Then the Indian pulls the salmon to the shore by means of the short line tied to the shaft of the spear.

Often at this time of year they also fished with a net in the river at night. The canoe was anchored at a deep spot near the shore by means of a pole driven into the bottom of the river. One of the corners of the net (four by four meters) was fixed to this pole. The mesh of the net was about ten centimeters. The other upper corner of the net was tied to a pole so that the net, hanging downward when weighted with stones, reached like a wall across the current. The Indians fixed bundles of mussel shells and crab claws to the net, which by their clattering told the Indians, who often slept in the canoe, that a fish had gotten into the net and was fighting against it.

In the summer also the Indians caught some salmon in the river, the fish having stopped there on their way back to the sea. The Indians closed off the river by a lattice structure between the banks at shallow narrows, above which the water was deeper. The lattice reached about one-half meter above the surface and the openings were so narrow that no grown fish could get through. The shallow water prevented the fish from jumping over the barrier. The salmon collected in the pools under the high banks, where the Indians,

Decline and Fall: The American Invasion » 177

cautiously coming up in the stream, speared them with salmon spears.

Other fish were also caught in the sea, but this fishing was done only as a sideline, because these species were not plentiful. In the summer, when the sea was calm, the Indians fished with the wall net described above (the mesh was a little smaller), attached between the canoe and several kelpheads, which, being filled with air, always floated on the surface. The net was left out for several hours while the tide was rising. By that time there would usually be one to three fish in the net, catfish or a smaller fish, like a carp, which had beautiful sky-blue and golden-yellow stripes. (These fish are said not to spawn but to give birth to living young.)

At low tide the Indians wade through the pools left in the cliffs to entice fish from under the stones by means of stone lilies (*Encrinita*) taken out of their shells and fixed to willow sticks. The fish are then caught in small handnets. In the spring, schools of herring-like fish, which remain in these pools, are caught by the women in carrying baskets.

The most important product of these, next to the salmon, was the common edible mussel, which were found, in spite of the waves, attached to the coastal cliffs and rocks, and were collected at ebbtide by the women. When the sea was calm, the men rowed out to rocks farther out in the sea, where these mussels were found in greater numbers and also larger size (up to ten centimeters). Sometimes whole canoeloads were brought home. A stick, shaped like a chisel on both ends, was used to pry the mussels off the rocks where they grew in groups or massed. The stick was made of the very hard and tough wood of the redberry bush.

The huge piles of mussel shells near the village have already been mentioned. From these mussel shells one could recognize the location of an earlier village, situated on the first small tributary on the righthand bank of the Little River.[7] There was no other trace of this village. South of this river, in the fine sand of the beach, one could find a thin-shelled, yellow-skinned bivalve, about ten centimeters long, two fingers high, and one finger thick. Its tender and tasty body had a trunklike proboscis. These animals buried themselves in the sand; their position could be detected by the small, watery eruptions of sand which appeared at ebbtide when one stepped near them. These eruptions betrayed their presence and the animals could be dug up very easily.[78]

There were only a few cockles, a kind of scallop (Pecten). These and the sea-urchin—the yellow, roelike inside of which was eaten raw—and other shellfish played a very minor role in the home of the Indian.

The sea-crab (sea-spiders) invaded the salty water of the estuary of the Little River in great numbers at the time they got new shells. The crabs would then be speared with pointed sticks, the Indians wading knee-deep or even up to their chests in the water. The crabs were thrown into a sack or a net, which was soon filled. Instead of hard shells these crabs had soft skins.

The meat of the elk, the seal, sea lion, and other sea animals, was an important food although it was not procured regularly. These animals were deliberately hunted, whereas otters, bears, and wild geese were considered chance game. The elk was stalked carefully and killed with arrows. On much-used trails in the forest the Indians trapped the elk by means of snares. These nooses, from five to eight meters long, consisted of willow twigs twisted together to almost the thickness of an arm. Seals and various sea mammals were hunted with canoes on the rocks far out in the sea. The Indians landed carefully in order to surprise the sleeping animals, harpooned them with the seal harpoon, or killed them with arrows. Later on they used the much more effective rifle. The usually peaceful and shy brown bears, like the wild geese and ducks, were not especially hunted. Indians tried to kill the ducks and other small game by throwing rocks or sticks if these, as the saying was, came their way. Children also set up traps near the village, marking the runs and burrows of the small rabbit with sticks. If the animal entered the run, it would loosen a board weighted down with stones, which killed the animal.

15. The whole tribe was later supposed to have been sent, with several other tribes, to an Indian reservation in the north. There, exposed to the trickery and oppression of unscrupulous agents who

think only of their own profit, deprived of its freedom and occupation and its familiar way of living, one tribe after another goes toward its early end. The time is not far away when the knowledge of a whole race of people will be based only on archaeological exploration and the reports of contemporary observations."[70]

TSURAI VILLAGE, 1851–1916

TSURAI is a microcosm of the fate of the California Indians who lived in the thousands of villages and hamlets all over the state before the coming of the white men. The advent, in numbers, of Caucasians to Trinidad Bay placed the natives in intimate daily contact with an alien culture and a people who regarded Indians as inferiors. The Indians were exploited in various ways, and their native way of life was disrupted. The old social and economic system declined as the result of the impact of the newly introduced Caucasian cultural values. Intermarriage, diseases, whisky, pay for goods and labor, and a hundred other factors, all contributed to the breakdown of the Indian culture.[80] To secure desirable white man's manufactures such as clothing, lumber, nails, axes, whisky, guns, and the like, the Indians were forced to do whatever they could to secure the money needed and were thereby placed in the role of competitive laborers. Some people, probably the young and progressive individuals for the most part, moved away to near-by white towns or perhaps to the Klamath River villages. The population of Tsurai diminished during the second half of the nineteenth century until, in 1900, only the older people remained attached by bonds of memory, tradition, and homesite to the place of their forefathers.[81]

In the summer of 1949 efforts were made to secure from living Indians some details about the last inhabitants and the final abandonment of the site. The accompanying map (map 5) made on the spot in the presence of and with the help of several older Indians shows the location of the several houses and their owners about 1900. These owners were: Old Jennie, Old Mau, Wild Annie, Blind Tom, Humpback Jim, Old Tsurai, Oscar, Old Willie (pl. 10), Old Pete, and Elizabeth Warren. Each house was named—a good Yurok custom—and some of these names were recorded more than forty years ago by Waterman.[82] Unfortunately most of them are now forgotten, but it is possible to associate a few house names with those of the last occupants.

Waterman's plan of Tsurai village, drawn about 1906, is shown

Decline and Fall: The American Invasion

here in map 1. The solid outlines represent houses which were still standing in his time; the dotted outlines are former house sites. The arrows point out the position and location of the entrances. Waterman's plan and ours (map 5) show little similarity either in contour lines or in house locations. We are inclined to accept our map as more accurately representing the actual situation about 1900 for the reason that our map was made with surveying instruments. The house locations shown by us were based upon actual visible remains of the Indian houses whose owners were named on the spot by people who had lived in the village before its abandonment. Waterman's list of house names (arranged by number on his plan) together with the few names of occupants we were able to determine are given below.

No. on map	*House name*	*Occupant ca. 1900*
1	———	———
2	Wónu, "uphill"	———
3	Orígok	———
4	Tsurai	Old Tsurai
5	Ká'ukuts	———
6	Ote'tkol	———
7	Wohke'ro, "pepperwood"	Old Pete
8	Hike's, "downhill"	———
9	Wo'gi, "in the middle"	———
10	Me'kwer, "little"	Old Mau
11	Hita'u, "in the ocean"	———
12	Owr'grn, "where they gather rushes"	———

Waterman's map of Tsurai shows two sweathouses (A, B) and four house pits (dotted-line rectangles nos. 1, 3, 5, 6) without standing structures. Our informants could remember only one sweathouse, named Ergr-rk and owned by Old Mau. If only one of the two on Waterman's map is correct, it is probably sweathouse A. The sweathouse shown on map 1 was pointed out to us by Indians and was excavated by us in 1949.

Between Blind Tom's house and Old Mau's home was a circular

pit where the Brush Dance[83] was held. The last dance was held there in 1907 and 1908. Although the whole area formerly occupied by the site is now covered with a dense growth of trees and brush, it was, as late as 1900, kept cleared of growth except for a huge pepperwood tree which still stands. This tree was sacred, and was called by the natives "bad." If aromatic angelica root was burned beneath its branches and a person prayed for rain, the rain would come in two days according to the Indians. Children were warned to stay away from this tree lest bad luck befall them. If an infant died, the mother, after an interval of five days, hung the cradle in its branches. Near the tree, where the creek was dammed, was the waterhole for washing or drinking water.

Old Mau seems by all accounts to have been the big man of the village. It was he who lived, as late as 1906, in the last remaining native house, of the type drawn by Bruff, and who owned the sweathouse where the men gathered.

One observation connected with the genealogies collected by us, but not presented here, concerns the places from which husbands or wives came to live at Tsurai. The man called Old Tsurai was a native of the town called Meta on the Klamath River. Old Pete's father was from Oketo, a town at the southern end of Big Lagoon. Wild Annie's father was from a village near Gold Bluff, and one of her husbands was from Mad River, to the south, in Wiyot territory. Blind Tom's wife was from Tsapekw on Stone Lagoon, and one man was remembered for having had five wives, each from a different place. This shows clearly that the Yurok tribe as a whole must have exhibited a complex system of interrelated families so that people from distant river and coastal towns were bound by ties of kinship.

As the young people moved away and left only the old people at Tsurai, the population decreased, and one by one the dozen houses were abandoned. One man who as a youth had lived in the village said, "Tsurai just died out." The last house occupied was that of Humpback Jim who died in 1913 or 1914. His wife lived until 1916 when she was removed, shortly died, and was buried elsewhere.

Sic transit gloria Tsuraiensis.

APPENDIX

INDIAN PLACE NAMES
IN TRINIDAD BAY

Indian Place Names in Trinidad Bay

(This listing of some seventy-five place names, for use with map 6, p. 100, is based largely on T. T. Waterman's *Yurok Geography*, AAE, Vol. 16 [1920].)

1. *Otswi'gen,* "where you talk." A group of flat rocks wherein resides a spirit who will help a person if he tells his troubles to the spirit.
2. *Olū'p,* "sound of breakers." A spot on the bluff (on the old baseball grounds) where the sound of breakers can be heard very clearly.
3. *Trgwr'g.* A sea stack just offshore.
4. *E'go.* A beach used as a camping spot for men going out for fish or sea lions.
5. *Rä'yip,* "on the other side, beyond." A pebbly beach.
6. *Mewome'kwel.* The level area just north of Trinidad Head.
7. *Pe'meole'gelin,* "grease where it hangs." A niche in the rock. The word *peme* means whale blubber.
8. *Oträ'hko,* "where it drops or trickles." The name refers to a cave into which people went in order to become wealthy. If one drop of water fell on the person he would soon become rich. If two drops fell on him he was doomed, since the rock closed behind him. A myth recounts how one man who possessed great "power" went into this cave and two drops fell on him. He was so powerful (in a spiritual sense) that he walked through solid rock and came out near where the wharf stands.
9. *Ho'ktkel.* A place where the people practiced shooting the bow and arrow.
10. *Mä' äq,* "he sits forever," or "he does not move." The name refers to a point of rocks. A man once went to this spot to "cry" for luck. (The Yurok continually sought means of acquiring more wealth in the form of dentalium shells.) One day as the man sat weeping and calling on the supernatural beings to help him to become rich, he saw "money" (dentalium shells) in the water as numerous as sardines. He sat there continually, refusing to go away, and finally turned to stone, now the pile of rocks. (This kind of myth is very common among the Yurok.)
11. *Tsure'wa,* Trinidad Head. The name comes from Tsurai, "mountain." Waterman thinks the name is not merely descriptive, since it is only a knoll of rock connected with the main shore by a low and narrow neck. At the top of the head there is said to be a hole in the rock with a spring in it.
12. *Onego',* "where it meets." A small inlet where the waves meet in a chasm or cleft and sweep against the rocks.
13. *Lege'pau,* "cache." The name refers to a small cave in the rocks where

the people used to secrete harpoons and other tackle when they went away from Trinidad. It was probably the local equivalent of a safe-deposit vault.

14. *Tmerumi'loloo'*, "watches the people." The reference is to a particular spot on the side of Trinidad Head where there lived a one-legged spirit who "kept track of everything people did." In Waterman's time (1909) the natives said they were "unclean" (in a spiritual sense and as a result of not observing the sacred taboos) and could not see this spirit, though they knew he still lived there.

15. *Ne' mä^w*, "adze." A projecting point of land shaped like the Yurok adze which has a curved stone handle.

16. *Ko'ixkulole'gwo m*, "perforated stone where it is covered." The spot is a cave just below the lighthouse. People took aromatic angelica root into the cave and put it into a pool of water in a recess of the cavern. The water would whirl when this was done. If this root (used in many religious and ceremonial connections) was employed by the person in some undertaking, it would turn out well.

17. *Pu'uktikoo'lo*, "albino deer where he stands." This name refers to a rock just below the cave described as no. 16. The reference may be to the color of the rocks, or their configuration, though the real reason is not known.

18. *Yu'lpets*, "white." Pilot Rock in Trinidad Bay.

19. *Hryrmr'is*, "corner." Place where the shore of Trinidad Head turns back toward the shoreline of the bay proper.

20. *Tsrhr'lik*, from *tsr'hr*, "sea-lion harpoon." The name refers to a hole in the rock near the outer face of the head where people cached harpoons and other tackle (cf. no. 13).

21. *Olega'^{w}*, "where they come." A place near the end of the present wharf which got its name because objects continually drift ashore there.

22. *Uke'wan*, "his basket." A small beach below the cliff between Trinidad Head and the smaller point called Little Trinidad Head.

23. *Oto'hpa^w*, "where there is a passageway." On this promotory there is a natural archway through a point of rock.

24. *Kr'nitwo ol*, "chicken hawk his house." A promontory now called Little Trinidad Head. Chicken-hawk, a famous character in Yurok mythology, had his original home at this spot.

25. *Kr' nitwe yotsolep*, "chicken-hawk his boat where it lies." A rock in the surf which bears a resemblance to the rounded bottom of an overturned canoe. A myth recounts that when *Kr'nit* went away he turned his boat over and left it there. *Kr'nit's* wife was the ocean and was always talking and muttering. The Indians say, "and she is that way even yet."

26. *Ole'gel*, "here they get clay or earth." People came here to obtain a blue clay which was used like "soap" to whiten buckskin dresses.

Indian Place Names » 187

27. *Omi'ige*, "where they practice or imitate." Little girls went to this spot, on a small promontory, to practice the Brush Dance.

28. *We'tpaori'-gen*, "sea lion where he always sits." A rocky point said by the Indians to look like a sea-lion's head.

29. *Prlkwrk*, "gray, or yellow." A small rock in the surf.

30. *Oʾstse'gep*, "where they disembark." A rock lying just in front of the landing place on the beach of the village of Tsurai.

31. *Tsu'rai*, "mountain." The only permanent Indian village on Trinidad Bay. The Indian names for the tribe and village at Trinidad Bay merit brief discussion. Meyer calls the tribe *Allequa*, and Bruff gives their name as *Aliquois*. Modern linguists have recorded this word as *Olekwot*, meaning "Indian" or "person." Any Yurok, at Trinidad, along the coast to the north, and along the Klamath River, uses this word to refer to a person of his tribe. The name for the village is given variously as *Choli* (Bruff, 1851), *Kori* (McKee, 1851),[1] *Tschura* (Meyer, 1851), *Tsorei* (Loeffelholz, 1850–56), *Sho'ran* (Davidson, 1869),[2] *Tsurau* (Kroeber, 1925), and *Tsurai* (Waterman, 1918). In the summer of 1949 the present authors heard this word, from different Indians, as *Choris, Churai, Churay*. We have adopted Tsurai as our version, a word meaning "mountain" and applied by the Indians to the village near the base of Trinidad Head, also so named. The neighboring tribe to the south, the Wiyot, called Tsurai village *Dakachawayawik*.

32. *Ko'ilwroi*. A small creek bounding Tsurai village on the west.

33. *Ego'rotep*, "cooking basket where it stands." A rock outcrop near the creek (no. 32) which suggests in form the hemispherical cooking basket.

34. *Pego'hpo*, "split." A cleft sea rock.

35. *Liqo'menoyowek*, "bait where they leave." A flat sea rock where people left bait and fishing lines.

36. *Egole'pa*, "cache." Like no. 35.

37. *Sko' ona^w*, A flat rock in the bay.

38. *Nuu'xpoq*, "double." A big sea rock divided by a wide chasm. It is now called Prisoner's Rock by white men.

39. *Rpla'^w*. A flat rock in the bay.

40. *Maoi'qoro*, "round." A sea rock.

41. *Prxteq^w*, "storage basket." A rock half buried in the sand which resembles in shape a storage basket.

42. *Prqwr'^w*. The end of Trinidad beach where the cliff begins again.

43. *Ole'gep*. The word refers to the fact that this rocky point formed a warm shelter from the wind.

44. *He'woliwroi*. A creek. The word is said to mean large.

45. *Pema'ksole'ĝ*, "soapstone dish where they make." A quarry where soapstone occurred.

46. *Tso'owin*. A flat rock in the bay.

47. *Olo'xtsul*, "where they wet basket materials." The origin of the name is obscure; it refers to a rock in the bay the top of which is always awash in the sea.

48. *Okr'gro*, "where they always gather clams." (Clam, *keptsr'*) The name probably refers to a series of rocks and reefs extending out from shore that look like clam shells scattered about.

49. *Mr'rp*. A rock in the bay.

50. *So'xtsin*. A promontory extending into the bay.

51. *Tä'amoslo'*, "elderberry bush where it grows." This place is a rocky crag.

52. *So'xtsinwroi*. A creek just below the promontory (no. 50) of the same name.

53. *Teweorega*, "in front of where they pass." Place where the trail turns inland to avoid some rocky cliffs.

54. *Alo'n*. Rock at the inshore end of a reef.

55. *Yr'mr'k*, "crooked." A distant sea rock.

56. *R'lrgr*, "where they get Indian potatoes."

57. *Okne'get*, "where they always get arrow points." Once, in mythical times, someone was going to make the rock at this place into a place where the people could go to get arrow points, but the scheme fell through.

58. *Oke'ga*, "where people get angelica root." This root (*wo'lpei*) was widely used in religious ceremonies and prayers and was offered to the spirit by burning it in the fire

59. *Tepo'na*. A rock with a tree on it lying close offshore.

60. *Omi'moswaä'g*, "Hupa his rock." Two nearly submerged sea rocks once bought by a Hupa man from Trinity River from the people of Trinidad because he liked to eat mussels. According to the Tsurai people, this man came over every season to collect the mussels (*pi'i*).

61. *Qege'tuwrl*, "puma his tail." A long, low-lying sea rock which resembles, in the Indians eyes, the puma's tail.

62. *Tegwolaäg*, "oceanward rock."

63. *Kwi'gerep*, "sharp." A narrow sea rock.

64. *Poi'k*. A bird. This sea rock, said to have some reference to the nighthawk, may be either the haunt of some kind of bird, or suggest one by its profile.

65. *Ketke'rok*, "hanging down." A crag.

66. *Osürg*, "blowhole." A rock cave at water level filled by each advancing wave; the air compression inside forces out a burst of spray.

67. *Me'stek*, "meadow." A flat (Honda Landing) behind the cliff.

68. *Prhrtsr'k*. A rock in the water.

69. *Osro'n*. A crag.

70. *Rayipa'*, "on the other side," "beyond." A small rock in the water.

71. *Sre'por.* A former village site marked by an accumulation of clam and mussel shell and several saucer-shaped depressions marking old house sites. It overlooks the mouth of Little River and was probably anciently occupied by the Tsurai people, though there is no evidence for this hypothesis.

72. *Rtskrgr'n,* "everybody looked." A great rock on the land side of the mouth of Little River where, according to a myth, *Kr'nit* (Chicken-hawk) was going to build a fish weir. In defiance of the taboos connected with such matters, "everybody looked," and he never succeeded.

73. *Me'tsko.* Little River.

74. *Okso'lig,* "where he fell," or "where they painted him." Sun (*wonu'-sleg,* "overhead he goes") once fell down here, according to a Yurok myth. Raccoon and his brother painted his face and threw him back again into the sky.

75. *Okwe'ges,* "where people get strawberries." The sand dunes near the mouth of Little River.

NOTES

NOTES TO INTRODUCTION

[1] Henry R. Wagner, *Spanish Voyages to the Northwest Coast of America*, California Historical Society Publication (1929), p. 157.

[2] Henry R. Wagner, *Sir Francis Drake's Voyage Around the World* (San Francisco, 1926), pp. 156–158, 169; George Davidson (*Identification of Sir Francis Drake's Anchorage on the Coast of California in the Year 1579*, California Historical Society Publication [San Francisco, 1890], pp. 55–56), concluded that Drake sighted Trinidad Bay.

[3] On this see Robert F. Heizer, *Francis Drake and the California Indians, 1579*, University of California Publications in American Archaeology and Ethnology, Vol. 42 (1947), 255–258. (This series hereafter cited as AAE.)

[4] Adele Ogden, *The California Sea Otter Trade, 1784–1848*, University of California Publications in History, Vol. 26 (1941), 7. Vancouver in 1793 had secured here "some very inferior sea otter skins." P. Tikhmeneff (*Historical Review of the Origin of the Russian American Company*, Vol. 1 [St. Petersburg, 1861], p. 206), states that by 1817 the sea otter had been exterminated from Trinidad to the vicinity of San Francisco Bay.

[5] Ogden, *op. cit.*, pp. 161–162, 168.

[6] H. H. Bancroft (*History of California*, Vol. II: *1801–1824* [San Francisco, 1886], p. 80), states that the crew of the *Kodiak* saw neither sea otters nor natives in Trinidad Bay.

[7] Eugène Duflot de Mofras, *Exploration du territoire de l'Orégon, des Californies et de la Mer Vermeille, exécutée pendant les années 1840, 1841, et 1842*, Vol. II (Paris, 1844), pp. 36–37, pl. 15, of Atlas volume. Jonathan Winship's map of Trinidad Bay of 1806 (printed in Tebenkof's *Atlas of the Northwest Coast of America, Aleutian Islands and North Pacific* [St. Petersburg, 1852], subchart to Chart XIII), is obviously copied from that of Vancouver.

[8] Owen C. Coy, *The Humboldt Bay Region, 1850–1875* (Los Angeles, California State Historical Association, 1929), p. 34

[9] See A. J. Bledsoe, *Indian Wars of the Northwest—A California Sketch* (San Francisco, 1885); Coy, *op. cit.*, chaps. ix–xi; L. L. Loud, *Ethnogeography and Archaeology of the Wiyot Territory*, AAE, Vol. 14 (1918), 305–337.

[10] Sherburne F. Cook, *The Conflict Between the California Indians and White Civilization: I–III*, University of California Ibero-Americana: nos. 21–23 (1943).

NOTES TO SECTION I
The Prehistory of Tsurai

[1] A similarly notched sword is illustrated by George Catlin, *Letters and Notes on the Manners, Customs, and Condition of the North American Indians* (2 vols.; London, 1841), I, 99. It was collected from the Plains Indians in the 1830's, and its manufacture is either American or English, probably the latter. Our Trinidad knives, of similar pattern, are therefore probably introduced by sea-otter skin traders carrying British-made trade goods during the fur-trade period as defined here.

NOTES TO SECTION II
Discovery and Exploration, 1775–1800

[1] Another account was published by A. J. Baker and H. R. Wagner, "Fray Benito de la Sierra's Account of the Hezeta Expedition to the Northwest Coast in 1775," *California Historical Society Quarterly*, Vol. IX (1930), 201–242. (This quarterly hereafter cited as *CHQ*.)

[2] For the background of this and other explorations, see Henry R. Wagner, "The Last Spanish Exploration of the Northwest Coast and the Attempt to Colonize Bodega Bay," *CHQ*, Vol. X (1931), 313–345. Also participating in the 1793 expeditions was Martinez y Zayas who drew a chart of Trinidad Bay; Zayas' map is only a copy of the Hezeta map of 1775 (see map 2).

[3] Fray Francisco Palóu (*Relación Historica de la Vida y Apostólicos Tareas del Venerable Padre Fray Junípero Serra* [Mexico, 1787], pp. 162, 170–172), reproduces a letter from Viceroy Bucareli to Fray Serra dated January 20, 1776, in which he says, "The Port of Trinidad discovered by Don Bruno Heçeta invites us to found an establishment..." Nothing came of his proposal to settle the harbor of Trinidad, largely because of the untimely death of Bucareli and the disinterest of his successor in the project.

[4] The "French Chart" is that of Jacques Nicolas Bellin, either the edition of 1755 or 1766.

[5] Bodega (*Comento*) says "possession was taken on the beach with the formalities that the Viceroy advised in his instructions and the place was named Puerto de la Trinidad."

[6] Bodega (*Comento*) adds that feathers were worn in the hair.

Notes » 195

[7] These "bands" may be marks for measuring shells of the dentalium used as currency.

[8] Bodega (*Comento*) says the Indians call these basketry caps *Corás*. A typical Yurok basketry hat was collected by Hewett of Vancouver's *Discovery* in Trinidad Bay in 1793. It is shown here on page 000, figure 3. J. Goldsborough Bruff (*Gold Rush* [New York, Columbia University Press, 1944], Vol. I, 428), shows another that he sketched in 1851. L. M. O'Neale (*Yurok-Karok Basket Weavers*, AAE, Vol. 32 [1932], 1–184), shows a number of more modern examples. They are primarily an article of women's dress of the Yurok and other northwestern California tribes.

[9] The custom of wearing flowers in the hair was widespread in the West. See A. H. Gayton, "Culture-Environment Integration: External References in Yokuts Life," *Southwestern Journal of Anthropology*, Vol. 2 (1946), 256.

[10] These "pins" may be of bone, as stated, or possibly long dentalium shells which are white and of smooth surface.

[11] Probably *Viburnum* pits.

[12] Either broken dentalium shells, too short to have value as money, or shells of the olivella with ground-off spires.

[13] No authoritarian chiefs, such as this statement implies, were known among the Yurok.

[14] Bodega (*Comento*) says that "more than two hundred and fifty Indians were seen."

[15] A year-old child shooting a bow and arrow seems impossible—the Spanish probably underestimated the boy's age. The point is clear, however, that very young children learned the use of the bow.

[16] It is probable that the Spaniards confused the mourning of a dead native with the subsequent sweating (a ceremonial cleansing or purification following contact with a corpse) in the sweathouse where a fire was built to generate heat. The Yurok are not known to cremate the dead. The account states that after they entered the house they saw no evidence of cremation.

The "house of the captain" clearly means the sweathouse. This house probably belonged to the village headman who was the richest person but it was for the use of all adult males.

[17] These iron knives are mentioned in other accounts of this expedition and by later observers. One example excavated from the village site of Tsurai is shown in plate 2, *k*. T. A. Rickard, ("The Use of Iron and Copper by the Indians of British Columbia," *British Columbia Historical Quarterly*, Vol. 3 [1939], 25–30), believes the Trinidad knives were made from iron salvaged from drift wreckage. Bodega (*Comento*) says the Indians were given knives and hoops of iron.

New Mexico is so far distant that it can scarcely be supposed to have been the source of the iron. Also it lies to the south. The Indians were probably correct in indicating that some tribes to the north had iron and that it was passed south by trade. A wrecked ship along the coast of Oregon, Washington, or British Columbia might have supplied sufficient iron for the various coastal tribes for years.

[18] The growing of tobacco and its smoking in stone-bowled or tubular wooden pipes is shared by most Indian tribes of northwestern California. Hewett (surgeon's mate on Vancouver's *Discovery*) collected a stone tobacco pipe at "Trinidada" in 1793. It is illustrated and described by O. M. Dalton, "Notes on an Ethnographical Collection from the West Coast of North America... Formed during the Voyage of Captain Vancouver, 1790–1795," *Internationales Archiv für Ethnographie,* Vol. 10 (1897), pl. 15, fig. 5.

The Yurok smoke only tobacco planted and tended by them, though the wild tobacco plant of their territory is of the same species (*Nicotiana bigelovii*). For details, see A. L. Kroeber, *Salt, Dogs, and Tobacco,* University of California Anthropological Records, Vol. 6 (1941), 16.

[19] Probably elk. There is no record of buffalo in this region.

[20] This is a reference to the redwood or Sequoia. A vara is 32.91 inches. Sixty varas would equal about one hundred and sixty feet.

[21] Trinidad Bay is situated in 41° 3' north latitude, and 124° 8½' west longitude. It lies 18° 49½' west of San Blas.

[22] Pilot Rock.

[23] Little River. Fray Palóu says this river was named "El Principio" (Herbert E. Bolton, ed., *Historical Memoirs of New California,* Vol. 4 [Berkeley, University of California Press, 1926, p. 12]).

[24] Hezeta notes here again that the cross was set up on the beach. Cf. note 5.

[25] Probably Little River. *Tortolas* means turtle doves.

[26] If the fourth quadrant is northwest, the doors of the houses faced southeast.

[27] Hezeta is here describing the subterranean sweathouse. For an illustration of the sweathouse, see plate 8.

[28] Polygyny (or polygamy) was possible if a man was rich. Wives were purchased, and only the well-to-do could afford more than one. Since chiefs were always rich men, the idea that these alone could have more than one wife is an understandable error.

It is of interest that in 1949 we were told of a former rich man of Tsurai who had five wives. He was the great-grandfather of Axel Lindgren who now lives in Trinidad, and the father of Old Mau's wife. It seems probable that Loeffelholz makes reference to this man. If so, we may further identify the young chief named Largo, mentioned by Bruff in 1851, as the son of this much married chief.

[29] A *tuesa* is 1.672 meters or 66.3566 inches.

[30] Little River.

Notes

[31] Here he refers to the mountain (Trinidad Head) with the cross.

[32] Probably smelt or small surf fish caught with X-shaped dip nets.

[33] *Dedos* means fingers. Campa may refer to the thrusting spear used by most California Indians.

[34] Apparently the cross was first set up on the beach (see the accounts of Bodega and Hezeta), and was then carried to the top of Trinidad Head where it was again set up in a permanent place at the spot shown on the Hezeta map (map 2).

[35] The Indians did not take it down, and it was seen in 1793 by Vancouver and again in 1817 by Corney who, however, says that he saw it "on shore."

[36] These two villages, somewhere in the vicinity of Trinidad, cannot be identified. The people may have been from the large town on Big Lagoon to the north or from as far south as Mad River.

[37] These are the seamen, José Rodriguez and Pedro Lorenzo, who are mentioned in Hezeta's journal. Since neither Hezeta nor Fray Miguel de la Campa mention the return of the second man, it seems that he was successful, and that, since the Indians were friendly, he probably settled in the village. If this supposition is correct, it would be of much significance in the subsequent culture history of this village. Rodriguez would then be the first Caucasian resident of California north of San Francisco Bay.

[38] The feast of Corpus Christi is celebrated on the Thursday after Trinity Sunday.

[39] By "two bows" is meant double-ended, Four varas is approximately eleven feet. De la Sierra adds that the canoes were "half-decked at stem and stern except the poop, which has a piece added on top to prevent the entrance of the waves." Campa says (ninth day) that four canoes held twenty-four men, or six men per canoe, a figure which seems about right. Kroeber states that in 1900 the standard canoe length was eighteen feet, and it may be assumed from this that steel tools secured from Caucasians permitted the making of larger canoes in the historic period.

[40] The B version says "bugles," by which tubular glass beads is meant.

[41] The B version says "careened." Boot-topping is defined by William Falconer (*An Universal Dictionary of the Marine* [London, 1776] no pagination), as "the act of cleaning the upper part of a ship's bottom ... by making the ship lean to one side, as much as they can with safety, and then scraping off the grass, slime, shells, or other material ..."

[42] The B version says "rings like these in the end of a musquet." They were probably pieces like those shown on page 10, figure 1, *h–i*.

[43] The B version says "black or blue."

[44] A piece of iron stamped with a letter of the alphabet obviously indicates a European origin of the metal. Where the original account states that the letter is £, the B version gives it as Ciii. The B version implies that metal arrow points

were thus marked, but the original clearly states that this was true of the iron swords.

⁴⁵ Pilot Rock.

⁴⁶ The wording indicates an open wood fire, perhaps built on sand or earth in the canoe. Possibly a torch is meant.

⁴⁷ Vancouver is correct. The Yurok house is similar to that of the Nootka of Vancouver Island, in that the dwellings are of split planks. Such houses are distributed on the Pacific shore from Cook Inlet southward to the territory of the Wiyot tribe of Eel River

⁴⁸ The reference here is to a sweathouse.

⁴⁹ The visitors were probably members of the Wiyot tribe who lived at or near the mouth of Mad or Little rivers.

⁵⁰ Fire or smoke signaling was practiced by most of the California Indian tribes.

⁵¹ One of these bows was purchased by George Hewett, surgeon's first mate on the *Discovery*, and later came into the possession of the British Museum. It is illustrated and described as thirty-six inches long, sinew backed, and with a leather thong wrapped about the center (pl. 7). See C. H. Read, "An Account of a Collection of Ethnographical Specimens Formed During Vancouver's Voyage in the Pacific Ocean, 1790–1795," *Journal of the Royal Anthropological Institute*, Vol. 21 (1891), 99–100; also Paul Schumacher, "Methods of Making Stone Weapons," *Bulletin of the United States Geological and Geographical Surveys of the Territories*, Vol. 3 (1877), 547–549, for the Yurok method of flint flaking.

⁵² Noted also by Shaler in 1804. Extreme tooth wear, a result of mastication of gritty foods, is common along all California Indians. See R. Leigh, *Dental Pathology of Aboriginal California*, AAE, Vol. 23 (1928), 399–440.

⁵³ "Punctations" may mean visible scarification, though plain tattooing would be expected and be remarked on, as it was by subsequent visitors to Trinidad Bay.

⁵⁴ Eliza probably already knew of the fact that Vancouver had called at Trinidad three months before. It is curious that Eliza does not mention the Spanish cross erected by Hezeta in 1775 and noted as seen by Vancouver.

NOTES TO SECTION III
Exploitation: The Fur Trade, 1800–1849

¹ From this simple statement, it might be thought that the Trinidad natives had had previous contact with fur traders, though our researches have failed to yield evidence of such visitors between 1793 (Vancouver and Eliza expeditions) and 1804 (Shaler).

NOTES   » 199

[2] He perhaps means that the village was abandoned.

[3] The *Columbia* in 1817 experienced similar treatment, a natural "salutary effect."

[4] False hair is not otherwise known to have been used in arranging the coiffure of the Yurok male, although it is possible.

[5] The entire expanse of the site formerly occupied by the village of Tsurai is covered with shells of mussels and clams to a depth of several feet. The same situation appears north and south along the ocean shore in those places occupied in former times by Indians. The remains of the old village sites are simply ancient garbage dumps.

[6] The same method of fashioning iron was mentioned in 1775 by Fray Miguel de la Campa of the Hezeta expedition.

[7] A waistcoat of several thicknesses of tanned elkhide was commonly used in northwestern California as armor. It is effective in withstanding arrows, but would not, of course, give protection against musket balls.

[8] There is no other record of tattooing the tongue black. Chin stripes are mentioned by several observers. Meyer adds that a stripe is added every five years. For face tattooing of California Indians, including the Yurok and neighboring tribes, see A. L. Kroeber, *Handbook of the Indians of California*, Bureau of American Ethnology, Bulletin 78 (1925), pp. 77–78, fig. 45; Edward Sapir, "Hupa Tattooing," *Essays in Anthropology Presented to A. L. Kroeber* (University of California Press, 1936), pp. 273–277; Stephen Powers, *Tribes of California*, Smithsonian Institution Contributions to North American Ethnology, Vol. 3 (1877), figs. 10–18.

[9] The cross was probably the one erected by the Hezeta expedition in 1775. The story of the Spanish wreck and massacre of the crew has no known basis in fact.

[10] The Yurok villages often engaged in feuds, and this observation may refer to ordinary precautions to prevent contacts between two feuding groups.

[11] The structural feature of ribs is not otherwise mentioned by any observer. The Indians may have been trying to imitate the ribs of European small boats. A breadth of six to eight feet for the redwood canoe is almost certainly too much.

[12] *I-equaw-ya*, "how do you do." Compare with Bruff (p. 114). Corney gives *chilese*, "barter" a native word which refers to "knife" according to Bruff (p. 114), and therefore a common object of Indian trade with Europeans. Modern Yurok would be *ayekwī*.

NOTES TO SECTION IV
Decline and Fall: The American Invasion, 1850–1916

[1] *Alta California,* July 8, 1850.

[2] *San Francisco Bulletin,* November 29, 1856. Account of a white man going to the rancheria near town (Tsurai) and raping a woman. The woman's son attacked him with a knife and mortally wounded him.

[3] The Yurok as a whole did not participate in these troubles. The Yurok, like the neighboring Hupa of Trinity River, did not permit the government to remove them to a reservation. In September, 1851, Redick McKee, acting as United States Indian Agent, met with the Indians of Trinidad Bay who numbered about fifty, gave them presents in the name of the President, and requested them to settle upon a reservation near the mouth of Eel River. The Indians refused, apparently through fear of being mistreated. U. S. Congress, Senate, *Report of Expedition Leaving Sonoma August 9, 1851 ... to the Klamath,* by Redick McKee. 33d Cong., spec. sess., Sen. Ex. Doc. 668 (Washington, 1853), p. 155.

In 1907 the U. S. Bureau of Indian Affairs made a census of Trinidad Indians preparatory to acquiring lands for the Trinidad rancheria which lies east of the town of Trinidad. The count showed thirteen families and thirty-four persons. Information from M. L. Robertson, District Agent, U. S. Office of Indian Affairs, Hoopa Agency.

[4] Trinidad Head was named "Gregg's Point."

[5] In March, 1850, the crew of the *Cameo* found the following inscription cut in a tree near the head of the bay:

> Lat. 41° 3′ 32″
> Barometer 29° 86′
> Ther. Fah. 48° at 12M
> Dec. 7, 1849. J. Gregg.

[6] Judging from this mention, the Indians must have been friendly. The Gregg party was a small one and much weakened by hardship.

[7] La Motte left San Francisco on March 20, 1850, on the *Laura Virginia* bound for the Trinity River gold mines. Trinidad Bay had only been rediscovered by the *Cameo* on February 16, 1850. The *Laura Virginia* entered the bay only three months after Josiah Gregg's visit.

[8] Compare with A. L. Kroeber, *The Languages of the Coast of California North of San Francisco,* AAE, Vol. 9 (1911), 423. R. B. Dixon and A. L. Kroeber, "Numeral Systems of the Language of California," *American Anthropologist,* Vol. 9 (1907), 663–690.

NOTES

[9] The author is confused. The wedges were of wood or antler, and the mauls were of stone.

[10] This is a brief and clear description of the cooking method called "stone boiling" practiced by all the aborigines of California.

[11] A deerskin mantle, as attested by several earlier observers, was standard dress for men.

[12] These special senses of the Indians are, within reasonable limits, only examples of individual development, and not the mark of a different order or type of inherited sensory abilities.

[13] The use of gestures, also described by Loeffelholtz, is not known to be an original California Indian culture trait. Gesture communication was probably developed after contact with Caucasians. Compare *chicano* with *chicoitz* (Bruff) and *chilese* (Corney).

[14] Compare W. Wallace, "Hupa Child-Training—A Study in Primitive Education," *Educational Administration and Training* (Jan., 1947), 13–25.

[15] Most California Indians burned over the land each year in fall or spring. This burning kept down the brush growth, made for easier travel, and the new grass attracted game.

[16] The Yurok language has never been fully studied and published. J. W. Powell ("Linguistic Families of North America," Bureau of American Ethnology, *Annual Report:* 7 [1891]), classified Yurok as of Weitspekan stock or family. Somewhat earlier six Yurok vocabulary lists were published by Powell in the appendix of Stephen Powers' *Tribes of California*, Smithsonian Institution Contributions to Knowledge, Vol. 3 (1877), 460–473. Edward Sapir, in 1913, showed that the Yurok language, together with the Wiyot, spoken immediately to the south, was identifiable as a member of the important North American stock called Algonkian ("Wiyot and Yurok, Algonkian Languages of California," *American Anthropologist*, Vol. 15 [1913], 617–646). Additional details on the Yurok language were presented by Kroeber, *op. cit.*, pp. 414–426. A large body of linguistic data collected by A. L. Kroeber and T. T. Waterman remains unpublished. Kroeber says (*Handbook of the Indians of California*, Bureau of American Ethnology, Bulletin 78 [1925], 15), that there were two Yurok dialects, one spoken south of Big Lagoon on the coast (this would include Tsurai), and the other along the ocean shore to the north and up the Klamath River. The southern coast dialect was called *nererner*.

The word given by Bruff for elk (*mar-wich*) is from Chinook Jargon. In this vocabulary the words in square brackets are modern renderings of the less accurate renderings given by Bruff.

[17] *Choli* is the same word as Tsurai and, as Waterman points out, means "mountain," the word for Trinidad Head.

[18] *Aliquoi* is variously rendered. *Alikwa* or *Olekwo'l* is perhaps the more correct orthography and means "Indian person." The native words in square brackets are from A. L. Kroeber's linguistic recordings.

[19] This description is to be seen written on the side of Bruff's sketch of the grave of a woman (pl. 8, top). The description actually refers to another picture—shown here in plate 7, top.

[20] This description was written by Bruff on the bottom of one of his sketches and refers to the same incident and grave (pl. 7, top).

[21] Owen C. Coy, *The Humboldt Bay Region, 1850–1865* (Los Angeles, California State Historical Association, 1929), p. 51, states that Luffelholz (locally called Luffenholz, i.e., Loeffelholz) erected a sawmill at Little River in 1851.

[22] For a summary of data concerning Indian physical types, see E. W. Gifford, "Californian Indian Types," *Natural History,* Vol. 26 (1926), 50–60.

[23] This is "papoose," a word originally from the Algonkian Indian language which was spread very widely in North America.

[24] The word "squaw" is also from the Algonkian Indian language.

[25] There is a record of bows of this heavy type used by the Maidu tribe of the Sierra Nevada region for hunting bear.

[26] Compare this with the account of Indian marksmanship given by Loeffelholz on p. 155.

[27] Beliefs in blood sacrifice do not ring true for California Indians. Meyer may have allowed his imagination too free a rein, or thought that red designs were painted in blood.

[28] Here the author has apparently confused "stone boiling" of liquids in baskets as a baking process.

[29] Meyer here refers to the dentalium shell money of the Yurok. He is incorrect as regards their size and color. They are hollow, slightly curved, white, and small in diameter with one end slightly larger than the other. They did come from the north by intertribal trade, their source being among the Kwakiutl of Vancouver Island, British Columbia. Cape Mendocino was about the southern limit of the use of dentalia currency. The use of "Indian money" by white traders in dealing with the natives is of interest.

For a discussion of the valuations of dentalium shell currency, see A. L. Kroeber, *op. cit.,* pp. 22–25. The number of shells on a string was the important fact, the longer shells being the most valuable. The longest shells measured two and a half inches and eleven of these made a string whose standard length was twenty-seven and a half inches. An eleven-shell string was worth $50; a twelve-shell string, $20; a fifteen-shell string, $2.50. Long and valuable shells were kept in elkhorn purses. One collected by Hewett, of the Vancouver expedition, at Trinidad in 1793, is shown here in figure 3, p. 15.

[30] These are crests of the pileated woodpecker.

[31] Meyer's observation is partly correct, his reasoning wrong. Kroeber (*op.*

NOTES » 203

cit., p. 44) explains this situation: "Births occurred among the Yurok and their neighbors chiefly in spring. This was, of course, not because of any animal-like impulse to rut at a certain season, as has sometimes been imagined, but because of highly specialized ideas of property and magic. The Yurok had made the just psychological observation that men who think much of other matters, especially women, do not often become or remain wealthy. From this they inferred an inherent antipathy between money and things sexual. Since dentalia money and valuables were kept in the house, a man never slept there with his wife, as already stated, for fear of becoming poor. The institution of the sweathouse where men worked and slept rendered this easily possible. In summer, however, when the cold rains were over, the couple made their bed outdoors; with the result that it seems natural to the Yurok that children should be born in the spring."

[32] That is, Requa or Rekwoi, the name of the Indian town at the mouth of the Klamath.

[33] This custom of wearing flowers plucked from the earth of relatives' graves is not reported by later observers. Indeed, the Yurok refuse utterly to smoke wild tobacco leaves because, so they say, it may have grown on a graveyard, or from seed produced on a graveyard. If Meyer's observation is correct, the difference may be in the function of the two plants. Altogether, Meyer's statement sounds improbable in the light of what is known about the Yurok.

[34] Again Meyer has set down cultural data which have not been otherwise recorded. Meyer was an acute and sympathetic observer, and some kernel of truth must lie in his account of transmigration, but it is difficult to separate the truth from the chaff of interpretation.

[35] Compare T. T. Waterman, *Yurok Geography*, AAE, Vol. 16 (1920), 191.

[36] The subtitle of this account reads: "Based on a manuscript left by the late Hans Friedrich Karl, Baron von Loeffelholz, and supplemented by Karl, Baron von Loeffelholz, K.U.K., Hauptman i.R." Further explanation is given in an extended footnote in the original publication: "This dissertation is based upon two manuscripts: first on an essay written by Baron von Loeffelholz, Reserve Captain, from his own recollections and notes and presented, together with some ethnographic objects and a human skull, to the K.U.K. Museum of Natural History in 1891; and second, on a much older manuscript written in 1857 by his father, the late Hans Friedrich Karl, Baron von Loeffelholz. This second manuscript was discovered only after the first had been submitted for publication, and did not reach the Museum until last year. The two manuscripts were combined in a single dissertation, with the approval of Captain von Loeffelholz. The great interest aroused by a truthful eyewitness account of the life of an Indian tribe which has since disappeared from the face of the earth [*sic*] justified making slight changes in the older manuscript and placing the additions made in the second account into an appendix. This has

necessitated several repetitions which were impossible to avoid unless one were willing to make a completely new work which would then not have had the importance of the original. In many cases these repetitions, given in different words, will be welcomed by the expert. It must be remembered that all references to time refer to the period before the year 1857. The illustrations are of the original objects donated by the Barons von Loeffelholz. The editors."

[37] The California Indians, according to most of the testimony of early observers, were unaggressive, mild tempered, and rather gentle people, and in these characteristics differed from many other American Indians who were of warlike disposition. Much of the aggressive spirit of North American Indians was acquired by contact with the white man brought about by the latter's westward movement from the eastern seaboard during the period 1700–1850. Many California tribes were forced to armed resistance for survival. This whole subject has been ably treated by S. F. Cook, *The California Indian and White Civilization:* I–III, University of California Ibero-Americana, Nos. 21–23 (1943).

[38] Actually the mission area was near the coast, and extended from Mission San Diego de Alcala (founded 1769) to Mission San Francisco de Solano at Sonoma (founded 1823) north of San Francisco Bay.

[39] The Spanish priests did, of course, so instruct the California natives.

[40] These remarks are certainly notable for their accurate assessment of the social problem posed by the presence of an underprivileged Indian minority in California at this early date.

[41] For Indian-Caucasian difficulties of the neighboring Wiyot, whose center lay at Humboldt Bay, see L. L. Loud, *Ethnogeography and Archaeology of the Wiyot Territory*, AAE, Vol. 14 (1918), 221–436. Indian "wars" in the northwest are treated by Coy, *op. cit.*, chaps. 9–11; and A. J. Bledsoe, *Indian Wars of the Northwest—a California Sketch* (Eureka, 1885).

[42] Dresses of this type are pictured by Arthur Woodward, "Some Tolowa Specimens," *Museum of the American Indian, Heye Foundation, Indian Notes*, Vol. 4 (1927), 137–150; Pliny E. Goddard, *Life and Culture of the Hupa*, AAE, Vol. 1 (1903), 1–88, pls. 5, 8.

[43] These pieces, often decorated with delicately incised geometric designs, are also used as delousers and head-scratchers. Examples are shown by Isabel Kelly, *The Carver's Art of the Indians of Northwestern California*, AAE, Vol. 24 (1930), 343–360.

[44] These would be the tribes of the Central Valley and Sierra Nevada who live in semisubterranean, earth-covered houses.

[45] The fireplace is a pit lined on four sides by flat rocks.

[46] These "huts" were probably small storage sheds.

[47] Widows were often taken as second wives by their dead husbands' broth-

Notes » 205

ers. This custom is called the levirate and was practiced by most California Indians.

[48] The "sitting cradle" of northwestern California. A. L. Kroeber, op. cit., pl. 35, illustrates cradles of this type.

[49] The "grass" is wild iris, *Iris macrosiphon*.

[50] The description seems to apply to a separate foreshafted arrow.

[51] This is sometimes said to be the best way of learning a native language, the process being called "marrying a dictionary."

[52] This observation has been generally made of California Indians. See George A. Pettitt, *Primitive Education in North America*, AAE, Vol. 43 (1946), 1–182.

[53] These words are from Chinook Jargon: *mowitsch, musch-musch, wau-wau, maḵamaḵ*. See George C. Shaw, *The Chinook Jargon and How to Use It* (Seattle, 1909).

[54] Compare this with the description and illustration of a grave given by Bruff.

[55] This incident is probably the one involving the Hupa of the lower Trinity River in 1856. See Coy, op. cit., pp. 45–46.

[56] A noose or snare set in a deer trail was commonly used in hunting deer.

[57] Such weirs were made on most of the larger salmon streams in Yurok territory. A famous weir is that made on the Klamath River at Kepel and described in detail by T. T. Waterman and A. L. Kroeber, *The Kepel Fish Dam*, AAE, Vol. 35 (1938), 49–80.

[58] See Chauncey S. Goodrich, "The Legal Status of the California Indian," *California Law Review*, Vol. 14 (1926), 83–100, 157–187.

[59] A statement which is obviously not true. The use of metal weapons by the Tsurai people as early as 1775 is mentioned in contemporary accounts.

[60] Neither Bering nor Cook was in this vicinity.

[61] This is probably the same sacred pepperwood tree mentioned by living Indians (see p. 182), otherwise called the bay or California laurel (*Umbellaria californica*).

[62] This Danish word, translated as "kitchen middens," refers to shell heaps which accumulate from the mollusks used as food.

[63] It is a fact that yellow glass beads are so rare as to be classed as practically absent in historic archaeological sites in California. Loeffelholz is speaking as a trader here, and undoubtedly his facts are correct.

[64] Rather than "gifts," the man was actually paying indemnity for an offense.

[65] The site named Srepor, No. 71 on map 6, may be the location of a seasonal camp of the Tsurai people.

[66] Probably buckeye (*Aesculus*) wood.

[67] Compare the account of Meyer.

[68] The Indian potato, *Brodaiea*.

[69] The pattern may have come from short Spanish broadswords. See plate 2.

[70] This, again, is a description of a separate foreshaft of wood attached to the end of the arrow.

[71] A bow which pulls one hundred and ten to one hundred and sixty-five pounds can be used only by a strong man. Either Loeffelholz has overestimated the strength of the Yurok bow, or later examples collected from Indians are weaker.

[72] Actually the Yurok had numerous types of polished stone tools, as archaeological and ethnological collections from prehistoric sites and surviving Indians demonstrate. Loeffelholz may mean that by the full historic period these were no longer in evidence, iron tools being in common use.

[73] The Tlinkit language is completely different from that of the Yurok (Zoreisch), and no advantage in reproducing this list is apparent. It has, accordingly, been deleted.

[74] These brief notes on sign language are extremely interesting. Since nothing of this kind is otherwise attested for the Yurok or any other California tribe, it is probable that gestures of this variety are the result of a development occurring in historic times in response to the need for communication between the Indian and the white man. This may not, however, be the case, and some effort should be made to ascertain whether such signs are an original feature of Yurok culture.

[75] Compare with Nos. 8, 14, 16 on map 6.

[76] The Yurok bury their dead in the extended position; the corpse is placed on its back. This position is not usual among California tribes.

[77] Here there may be a reference to the site of Srepor. If so the site was abandoned by the middle of the last century.

[78] This description probably refers to the razor clam *Siliqua patula*.

[79] This statement is completely true for the southern Coast Yurok for which the Tsurai village was a main center. The Yurok of the Klamath River still number several hundred, and include many persons who remember the old native culture.

[80] Cf. H. G. Barnett, "Culture Processes," *American Anthropologist*, 42, (1940), 21–48.

[81] The number of houses and persons at Tsurai seem to have fluctuated somewhat during the period of contact with the white man. The table below summarizes these data:

Observer	Year	Dwellings	Sweathouses	No. of persons
De la Campa	1775	6	1	
Vancouver	1793	4	1	About 54*
Eliza	1793			200†
Shaler	1804	About 12		Not over 100
McKee	1851			About 50
Loeffelholz	1850-1856	6 or 8		50 to 80
Bruff	1851	4	1	
Local Indians‡	1900	10		About 35
Bureau Indian Affairs	1907	(13 families)		34

* Vancouver counts six to seven persons per house, but includes the sweathouse in his total house count of five.
† May include visitors from neighboring villages. Cf. Vancouver's account.
‡ Information secured by the authors, summer 1949.

[82] T. T. Waterman, *Yurok Geography*, AAE, Vol. 16 (1920), 177-314, map 34. Reproduced here as map 1.

[83] For details see A. L. Kroeber, *Handbook of the Indians of California*, Bureau of American Ethnology, Bulletin 78 (1925), 61-62.

NOTES TO APPENDIX

[1] U. S. Congress, Senate, *Report of Expedition Leaving Sonoma August 9, 1851 ... to the Klamath,* by Redick McKee. 33d Cong., spec. sess., Sen. Ex. Doc. 668 (Washington, D.C., 1853), p. 155.

[2] U. S. Coast Survey. *Pacific Coast Pilot of California, Oregon and Washington Territory,* by George Davidson (Washington, D.C., 1869), p. 104.

www.ingramcontent.com/pod-product-compliance
Lightning Source LLC
Chambersburg PA
CBHW021707230426
43668CB00008B/750